365 WAYS TO COOK HAMBURGER

365
ways
to
cook
HAMBURGER

by
Doyne Nickerson

Doubleday & Company, Inc., Garden City, New York
1960

This book is dedicated to my mother-in-law,
DELPHINE FRANKLIN,
whose files turned up several interesting recipes she prepared
during World War I.

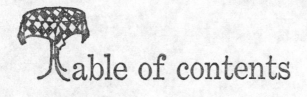

Table of contents

WEIGHTS AND MEASURES

3 teaspoons	1 tablespoon	½ ounce
2 tablespoons	⅛ cup	1 liquid ounce
4 tablespoons	¼ cup	2 liquid ounces
5 tablespoons plus 1 teaspoon	⅓ cup	2⅔ liquid ounces
8 tablespoons	½ cup	4 liquid ounces
16 tablespoons	1 cup	8 liquid ounces
2 cups	1 pint	16 liquid ounces

CAN SIZES

Buffet size	8 ounces	1 cup
Picnic size	10½ ounces	1⅓ cups
No. 211 can	12 ounces	1½ cups
No. 303 can	16 ounces	2 cups
No. 2½ can	26 to 28 ounces	3¼ cups
No. 10 can	6 pounds 9 ounces	12½ cups

PREFACE

The broiled or fried hamburger sandwich in a bun made its first appearance in 1903–1904 at the Louisiana Purchase Exposition (St. Louis Fair) along with the hot dog and the ice-cream cone.

Red meat, shredded with a dull knife, was eaten raw by the rugged citizens of Estonia, Finland, and Latvia prior to the Napoleonic era. The custom migrated to Hamburg, Germany, the largest seaport in Europe at that time. Prior to the turn of the century, sailors from Hamburg docking in New York City patronized the eating stands along the piers. They insisted that their beef be chopped and placed between buns so they could take it back aboard ship in bags.

From New York to St. Louis and on to the Back-yard Barbecue as we know it today, hamburger has become synonymous with twentieth-century America, more of it being consumed than any other one type of meat.

Many of the interesting recipes in this book have originated in foreign lands, others are present-day favorites. Still others were favorites of the past but have been forgotten in our present fast pace of food merchandising.

Should you desire to adapt any of the recipes to serve a larger number of people, increase the ingredients accordingly. For best results, it is suggested that seasonings be adjusted according to taste and that ingredients be mixed in smaller quantities and combined.

This book has been written with each of you in mind—bachelors, bachelor girls, newlyweds, small families, large families, those who like hamburger, those who are tired of hamburger cooked in the same old way, clubs, and church groups. You will find just the right recipe for just the right occasion, whether you are cooking on the hearth, in the woods, or on your favorite outdoor grill.

TURN THE PAGE AND EAT HEARTY.

tips on hamburger

Regular ground beef must not contain more than 25% fat.

Lean ground beef must not contain more than 12% fat.

Hamburger should be stored well refrigerated. It should not be stored for more than two days unless kept in a freezer. If stored in a freezer, use within two or three months.

Do not refreeze frozen hamburger once it has thawed.

Hamburger should be handled as little as possible, to keep it juicy and tender.

Pat hamburgers loosely into shape. Do not squeeze the juice out of them with a spatula while they are cooking.

Mix meat loaves by tossing together lightly with a two-tined fork.

The more times hamburger is ground, the more compact it becomes. Compactness is acceptable for meat loaves and meat balls.

A pound of hamburger makes 4 servings.

SANDWICHES
&
BARBECUES

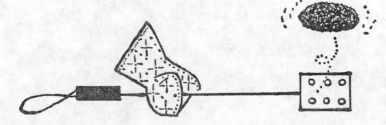

HAMBURGER BUNBURGERS

For basic hamburgers, mix 1 lb hamburger, ¼ cup minced onion, 1 tsp salt, ¼ tsp black pepper, and ¼ tsp monosodium glutamate. Form into 4 hamburgers, broil 3 inches from heat source until done the way you like them, and top with one of the following combinations of ingredients. Serve between toasted buns. Makes 4 hamburgers.

1. Thinly sliced raw onions, salt and pepper.
2. Grilled onion slices, catsup, salt and pepper.
3. Mix 2 tbsp melted butter, 1 tbsp lemon juice, dash of nutmeg.
4. Sliced fresh cucumbers, salt and pepper.
5. Mix 2 tbsp melted butter, 1 tbsp mustard, 2 tbsp minced ripe olives.
6. Sliced stuffed olives, thinly sliced tomatoes.
7. Mix 2 tbsp melted butter, 1 tsp minced onion, 1 tsp minced parsley, dash of Worcestershire, salt and pepper.

8. Fried green tomatoes, salt and pepper.
9. Mix 2 tbsp melted butter, 2 tbsp catsup, 1 tbsp prepared mustard, salt and pepper.
10. Sliced American cheese and catsup.
11. Mix 2 tbsp melted butter, 4 tbsp applesauce, and dash of nutmeg.
12. Thin tomato slices, mayonnaise, and crisp lettuce.
13. Piccalilli, mustard, salt and pepper.
14. 2 tbsp melted butter, 2 tbsp chili sauce, and 4 tbsp crumbled blue cheese.
15. 2 tbsp barbecue sauce mixed with 2 tbsp minced onion.
16. 1 tbsp horseradish, 2 tbsp catsup.
17. Mix 2 tbsp melted butter, 1 tbsp cream cheese, and 2 tbsp chopped chives.
18. Chili con carne or chili and beans.
19. Sliced dill pickles, catsup and pepper.
20. Cole slaw and caraway seeds.
21. Sautéed mushrooms and mayonnaise.
22. Mix 2 tbsp melted butter, 2 tsp prepared mustard, 2 tbsp chili sauce, and dash of chili powder.
23. Sliced radishes, salt and pepper.
24. Chopped green pepper, mayonnaise, salt and pepper.
25. Mix 2 tbsp melted butter, 2 tbsp prepared mustard, and 4 tsp minced parlsey.
26. French dressing and lettuce leaves.
27. Sauerkraut and pepper.
28. Mix 2 tbsp melted butter, 2 tbsp chopped dill pickle, and 1 tbsp minced onion.
29. Slices of Swiss cheese, catsup, and lettuce leaves.
30. Barbecue sauce and sliced tomatoes.
31. Mix 4 tbsp melted butter with ¼ tsp garlic salt.
32. Mix 4 tbsp melted butter with 1½ tsp anchovy paste.
33. Sliced avocado, mayonnaise, and lettuce leaves.
34. Mix 2 tbsp melted butter, 1 tbsp horseradish, and ¼ tsp garlic salt.
35. Grated Parmesan cheese, salt and pepper.

BARBECUED HAMBURGERS 1

Mix 1 tsp liquid smoke to 1 egg, slightly beaten. Combine with 1 lb hamburger, 1 tsp salt, and ¼ tsp pepper. Form into 4 hamburgers and broil till desired doneness. Serves 4.

BARBECUED HAMBURGERS 2

Sauté ½ cup chopped onion and ½ cup chopped green pepper in 1 tbsp cooking oil for about 3 minutes. Add 1 lb hamburger and cook until red color disappears. Add 2 tsp prepared mustard, 1 cup catsup, 1 tsp salt, and ¼ tsp pepper. Simmer for 10 minutes and serve in toasted buttered buns with a thin slice of onion. Serves 8.

BARBECUED HAMBURGERS 3

Sauté 2 cups chopped onion and ½ cup chopped green pepper in 2 tbsp cooking fat. Add 2½ lbs hamburger, crumbling it into small pieces as it browns.

Mix

1 8-oz bottle catsup	1 tbsp dry mustard
½ bottle chili sauce	2 tbsp vinegar
¼ cup brown sugar	1 tbsp salt

Mix sauce thoroughly, stir into browned hamburger, simmer for 1 minute, and serve over toasted buns cut in half. Serves 8.

BARBECUED HAMBURGERS FOR THIRTY

Brown 7 lbs crumbled hamburger in ½ cup drippings or cooking fat.

Add

3 qts canned tomatoes	2 tbsp salt
½ cup chili sauce	2 tsp liquid smoke
¼ cup Worcestershire sauce	

Simmer for 30 minutes, stirring occasionally. Spoon onto hamburger buns. Serves 30.

BISCUIT BURGERS

Mix

½ lb hamburger	½ tsp salt
2 tbsp minced onion	⅛ tsp pepper

Form into 6 thin patties 2½ inches in diameter. Mix biscuit dough according to directions on pkg and roll out ⅛ inches thick. Cut 3-inch circles and place a meat patty between 2 circles. Seal edges, prick tops, and bake on a baking sheet at 400° for 15 minutes. Serves 6.

BURGER DOGS

Mix

1½ lbs hamburger	1½ tsp salt
½ cup finely chopped onion	¼ tsp pepper
2 tsp prepared mustard	

Roll into patties the shape of hot dogs and wrap a slice of bacon around each, spiral fashion. Broil 3 inches from heat source until cooked to taste. Serve in hot dog buns with your favorite relish. Makes 10 to 12.

CHEESE BISCUIT BURGERS

Brown ¾ lb hamburger in 2 tbsp cooking fat. Add ½ cup chopped onion and ¼ cup diced celery and cook until soft. Stir in ¼ cup tomato paste, ½ cup water, ½ tsp salt, ¼ tsp chili powder, ½ tsp Worcestershire, and 1 2-oz can chopped ripe olives. Simmer for ten minutes.

In the meantime prepare biscuit mix according to directions on the package and cut into 16 circles about 4 inches in diameter. Put 8 of the circles on a greased baking sheet and put meat mixture in center of each circle. Top with other 8 circles and seal edges. Bake at 375° for 25 minutes until biscuits are brown. Place a slice of processed cheese on each sandwich and bake for 2 minutes more until cheese melts. Serves 8.

CHEESEBURGERS FOR TWENTY-FOUR

Mix

3 lbs hamburger	2 tsp Worcestershire sauce
1 cup chopped onion	2 tsp salt
½ cup chili sauce	½ tsp pepper

Spread on 24 hamburger buns and broil for 5 to 6 minutes. Place 1 slice American cheese on meat and broil till cheese melts. Toast top half of buns. Serves 24.

MEAT LOAF SANDWICHES

Spread bread slices with butter and mayonnaise. Arrange slices of any cold meat loaf on bread slice. Spread meat with horseradish and a lettuce leaf and top with bread slice.

LITTLE HAMBURGER PIZZAS FOR FIFTY

Mix and fry 6 lbs hamburger and 7 lbs pork sausage until brown. Toast 50 English muffins, sliced and buttered, in broiler or oven until brown. On each muffin half spread

| 1 tbsp tomato paste | ⅛ tsp oregano |
| 2 tbsp grated Cheddar cheese | ¼ cup meat mixture |

Top with sliced mushrooms and bake in hot oven at 400° for 7 minutes, or until cheese melts. Serves 50.

MEAL IN A SANDWICH

Split a loaf of French bread lengthwise and brush lightly with garlic butter. Place a grilled hamburger patty on one end of the loaf, next to that some sliced Swiss cheese, then slices of salami, sliced hard-boiled eggs and sliced ham. Top with sliced ripe olives, salt and pepper, and cover with top half of loaf. Serves 1 big man.

ENGLISH BURGERS

Brown 1 lb hamburger in 1 tbsp cooking fat. Add 2 tbsp catsup and 2 tbsp prepared mustard. Stir in 1 can condensed onion soup and 2 tbsp drained pickle relish. Simmer for 15 minutes. Serve over split toasted English muffins and top with American cheese melted in a double boiler. Serves 8.

VARIATIONS: Top with one of the following:
1. French-fried onion rings.
2. Chopped ripe olives and minced onion.
3. Tiny sardines.
4. Diced avocado.
5. Crumbled Roquefort cheese.

6. Diced tomatoes and minced green onions.
7. Chopped anchovies.
8. Crumbled crisp bacon.
9. Sautéed mushrooms.

OPEN HAMBURGERS FOR SIX

Mix

1 lb hamburger	1 tsp salt
½ cup minced onion	¼ tsp pepper

Spread 6 slices of bread with butter and a little mustard. Spread meat mixture to the edges of each slice and brush with butter. Broil 3 inches from heat source until done. Serves 6.

OPEN-FACED BURGERS

Toast a slice of sandwich bread on one side only. On the untoasted side, spread ¼ lb hamburger that has been seasoned with salt and pepper. Spread top of meat with prepared mustard, sprinkle with grated onion, dot with butter, and broil three inches from heat source for 7 minutes. Serves 1.

VARIATIONS: Eliminate the prepared mustard and top with one of the following:
1. Crumbled blue cheese.
2. Thin slices of tomato.
3. Thin slice of processed cheese.
4. Sliced stuffed olives.
5. ½ tsp horseradish.
6. Thin slice of sweet onion.
7. 2 tbsp chili sauce.
8. 2 tbsp baked beans.
9. Long slices of dill pickle.

10. Crisscrossed slices of Swiss cheese.
11. 2 tbsp sweet-pickle relish.
12. 1 tbsp spaghetti sauce, 1 slice mozzarella cheese and oregano.

OPEN DEVILBURGERS

Mix

1 lb hamburger	2 tsp prepared mustard
¼ cup minced onion	1 tsp salt
¼ cup chili sauce	¼ tsp pepper
2 tsp horseradish	¼ tsp monosodium
2 tsp Worcestershire sauce	glutamate

Toast 12 slices of bread and spread each slice with the meat mixture to the very edges. Broil about 3 inches from heat source for about 5 minutes or until done. Serves 6.

VARIATION: Top each sandwich with a slice of sharp processed cheese and broil until cheese bubbles.

THRIFTY BURGERS

Soak 2 slices of toast in ½ cup milk and mix with 1 lb hamburger. Add 3 beaten eggs, 1 tsp salt, and ¼ tsp pepper. Brown on both sides in a skillet and serve between toasted buns. Serves 8.

PARTY BURGERS

Mix

1 lb hamburger	2 tbsp Worcestershire sauce
¼ cup chopped onion	1 tsp salt
¼ cup water	¼ tsp pepper

Form into 6 patties and sauté in a skillet for about 3 minutes on each side. Serves 6.

DIETETIC OPEN HAMBURGERS

Mix

½ lb lean hamburger	½ tsp salt
½ cup minced onion	⅛ tsp pepper
½ tsp Angostura bitters	

Spread the meat mixture to the very edges of 4 slices whole-wheat bread. Broil 3 inches from heat source for 3 minutes. Remove from broiler and spread a little mustard on top of the meat and top with thin slices of tomato. Broil 2 minutes more. Makes 4 open sandwiches.

PATIO HAMBURGERS FOR FIFTY

Mix

12 lbs hamburger	4 tbsp salt
3 cups chopped onion	1 tsp black pepper

Place in 2 broiler pans and broil about 4 inches from heat source, stirring often, until well browned.

Mix

6 cups chopped onions	2 tbsp meat sauce
3 cups tomato paste	2 tsp oregano
3 qts cooked tomatoes	½ tsp Tabasco sauce
1 cup vinegar	⅛ tsp cayenne pepper
1¼ cups brown sugar	2 tsp liquid smoke
2 tbsp Worcestershire sauce	2 tbsp salt

Cook uncovered over low heat for 1 hour, stirring often.

Pour fat off meat and combine meat with sauce. Cook over low heat for 1 hour. Spoon onto hamburger buns. Serves 50.

RELISH BURGERS

Mix

1 lb hamburger	1 tsp salt
2 tbsp finely chopped parsley	¼ tsp pepper

Form into 8 patties 4 inches in diameter. On 4 of the patties place a thin slice of onion, slice of tomato, and a 3-inch square of American cheese. Cover with other 4 patties and seal edges. Broil for 10 minutes on each side and serve in toasted buns. Serves 4.

SAVORY BURGERS

Mix

1 lb hamburger	1 tsp prepared mustard
⅓ cup chopped onion	1 tsp salt
½ cup dry bread crumbs	¼ tsp pepper
2 tbsp Worcestershire sauce	½ tsp monosodium
¼ cup evaporated milk	glutamate
2 tbsp horseradish	

Form into 6 patties and fry in a skillet about 5 minutes on each side. Serve in hot buttered buns. Serves 6.

SOUR-DOUGH BURGERS

Mix

1½ lbs hamburger	1 tsp salt
½ cup finely minced onion	2 tbsp Worcestershire

Form into 4 patties to fit round slices of sour-dough French bread. Place meat on broiler rack and broil 2 inches from heat source for about 3 minutes, or until browned. Remove rack and turn meat. Sprinkle with a dash of oregano. Now place on the rack tomato halves seasoned with salt, pepper, and oregano. Place rack so that tomatoes are 3 inches from heat source and broil until meat is done the way you like it. Serve on toasted sour-dough French bread with the tomatoes on the side. Serves 4.

STUFFED BUNBURGERS

Hollow out the centers of 6 hamburger buns and mix the hollowed-out part with

1 lb hamburger	1½ 8-oz cans tomato sauce
¼ cup chopped onion	1 tsp salt
2 tbsp minced green pepper	¼ tsp pepper

Fill buns and bake at 375° for 20 minutes. Top with more tomato sauce and bake for 10 minutes longer. Serves 6.

GERMAN TARTARE

North Germany

Mix 1 lb very, very lean hamburger, ground twice, with 4 tbsp finely minced onion and 2 tbsp sweet-pickle juice. Form into 4 patties and make a depression in the top of each patty. Place the raw yolk of an egg in each depression and chill in the refrigerator for one hour. Serve on rye bread with green onions, radishes, pickles, and ale or beer. Serves 4.

HAMBURGER TARTARE 1

Spread ¼ lb lean raw hamburger on a large slice of buttered bread. Season with salt and black pepper. Top with a large slice of onion. Serves 1.

HAMBURGER TARTARE 2

Mix in a blender

½ lb hamburger   ½ tsp salt
2 Mexican hot peppers   ¼ tsp fresh ground black
1 small onion   pepper
1 tsp Worcestershire sauce

Spread on crackers to serve.

TURNOVER BURGERS

Sauté ½ cup chopped onion in 2 tbsp butter, then add

1 lb hamburger   ¼ tsp pepper
½ tsp garlic salt   ½ tsp monosodium
½ tsp sugar   glutamate
1 tsp salt

Cook for about 3 minutes and add 1 cup tomato sauce and ¼ cup of sour cream. Prepare biscuit mix according to directions on package and cut into 8 5-inch squares. Put ⅓ cup meat mixture on each square and fold diagonally to make triangles. Seal edges, prick top, and brush with butter. Bake on a sheet at 400° for 20 minutes. Makes 8 turnovers.

HAMBURGERS IN WINE SAUCE

Mix

2 lbs hamburger   2 tsp salt
1 cup chopped onion   ¼ tsp pepper

Form into 8 hamburgers, sprinkle lightly with flour, and fry in 2 tbsp butter until browned. Remove from skillet and keep warm. Fry 4 chopped mushrooms in the skillet for a few minutes, cover them with ½ cup boiling water, and thicken with 2 tsp flour. Add ½ cup white wine and heat but do not boil. Salt to taste and pour over hamburgers. Serves 8.

WESTERN RANGE BURGERS

Fry 4 slices of bacon crisp, drain and crumble. In 2 tbsp of the bacon fat, sauté ¾ cup sliced onion and ½ cup chopped green pepper until soft. Add 1 lb hamburger and cook until meat browns.

Add

2 No. 303 cans red kidney beans	½ tsp salt
	⅛ tsp black pepper
1 8-oz can tomato sauce	¼ tsp monosodium
Crumbled bacon	glutamate
2 tbsp chili powder	½ lb grated Cheddar cheese

Stir over a low heat until cheese melts and serve on 8 split toasted English muffins. Serves 8.

MEAT LOAVES

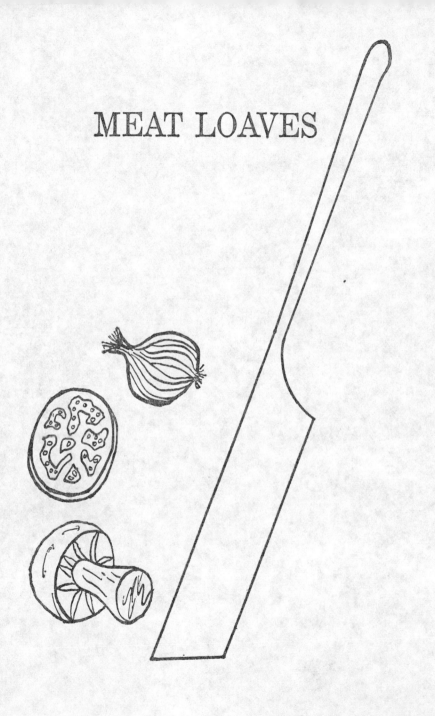

AVOCADO MEAT LOAF

Fry 4 strips bacon until crisp and remove from pan. In same fat, sauté ¾ cup diced celery, ½ cup minced green onions, 2 tbsp minced parsley, and ½ cup diced green pepper. When done, remove to a large bowl.

Add

1 lb ground veal	1 egg, slightly beaten
1 lb hamburger	2 tbsp flour
1 8-oz. can tomato sauce	1 large avocado, skinned
1 cup bread crumbs	and diced
2 cups fresh chopped	2 tsp celery salt
mushrooms	½ tsp pepper

Pack into a 5 x 5 x 9-inch loaf pan, sprinkle generously with paprika, and bake at 350° for 45 minutes. Remove excess fat from pan and bake for 45 minutes more. Serves 6.

BANANA MEAT LOAF 1

Mix

1 lb hamburger	2 tsp salt
1 cup bread crumbs	¼ tsp pepper
½ tsp paprika	1 tbsp chopped onion

Combine with ¾ cup mashed firm bananas mixed with ½ tsp dry mustard. Shape into loaf and bake in greased baking dish at 350° for 1 hour. Serves 4.

BANANA MEAT LOAF 2

Mix

2½ lbs hamburger	2 tsp prepared mustard
2 cups soft bread crumbs	2 tsp salt
4 mashed bananas	½ tsp pepper
¼ cup onion, chopped very fine	½ tsp monosodium glutamate

Shape into a loaf, top with strips of bacon, and bake at 350° for 1 hour. Ten minutes before loaf is done, place thick slices of banana on top of bacon. Serves 8.

BARBECUED MEAT LOAF

Mix

1 lb hamburger	3 tbsp horseradish
¾ cup bread crumbs	2 tbsp chopped onion
1 egg, slightly beaten	1 tsp salt
1 tbsp chopped parsley	⅛ tsp pepper
3 tbsp water	

Shape into loaf and set aside. To make barbecue sauce, mix and heat

1 tsp Worcestershire sauce	½ tsp dry mustard
½ cup chili sauce	⅛ tsp Tabasco
3 tbsp A.1. sauce	¼ tsp liquid smoke

Spread sauce over top of loaf and bake at 350° for 1 hour. Serves 4.

CALIFORNIA MEAT LOAF

Mix

1 lb hamburger	½ cup milk
1 cup corn flakes	¼ cup catsup
2 eggs, slightly beaten	1 tbsp Worcestershire sauce
1 tsp salt	1 cup raisins
⅛ tsp pepper	

Shape into loaf. Sprinkle ⅓ cup grated Cheddar cheese over top. Bake at 350° for 1 hour. Serves 4.

CHEESE-LAYERED MEAT LOAF

Mix

1½ lbs hamburger	3 eggs, slightly beaten
2 cups chopped onions	3 slices mild cheese
4 crushed crackers	1 tsp salt
1 cup seedless raisins	⅛ tsp pepper
¼ tsp nutmeg	

Place half of mixture in baking dish. Cover with very thin slices of mild cheese. Cover with rest of meat mixture. Shape into loaf. Bake at 350° for 1 hour. Serves 6.

VARIATION: Cover top with strips of bacon and let it crisp 10 minutes before serving.

BLACK BEAN MEAT LOAF

Mix

2 lbs hamburger   1 tsp salt
1 can condensed black bean   1 pkg dehydrated onion soup
  soup   1 egg, slightly beaten

Shape into loaf. Bake at 350° for 1½ hours. Serves 8.

,VARIATIONS: Place cheese slices over top. Place under
            broiler till cheese bubbles.
            Place thin tomato slices over top. Place under
            broiler until done.

CHILI HOT-TOP MEAT LOAF

Mix

1½ lbs hamburger   1 cup cracker crumbs
1 cup Parmesan cheese   1 egg, slightly beaten
½ cup chopped green pepper   ¾ cup milk
½ cup chopped onion   1 tsp salt

Bake in loaf pan at 350° for 45 minutes. Turn out loaf on a
baking sheet. Mix ¼ tsp hot sauce in ¾ cup chili sauce and spread
over sides and top of loaf. Bake at 350° for 15 minutes. Serves 6.

CLOVE-STUDDED MEAT LOAF

Mix

1 lb hamburger   1 tbsp cooking oil
¼ cup chopped onion   ½ cup water
¼ cup chopped green pepper   1 tsp Worcestershire sauce
½ cup bread crumbs   1 tsp salt
2 eggs, slightly beaten   ⅛ tsp pepper

Shape into loaf in baking pan and push 12 whole cloves into top of loaf and set aside.

Sauce:

1 8-oz. can tomato sauce	1 cup water
2 bay leaves	4 whole cloves
⅛ tsp dried crushed red peppers	⅛ tsp allspice

Cook for 30 minutes, remove bay leaves and cloves, and pour over top of loaf. Bake at 350° for 1 hour. Serves 4.

COTTAGE CHEESE MEAT LOAF

Mix

¾ lb hamburger	2 tbsp chopped green pepper
1 cup cottage cheese	3 eggs, slightly beaten
1 cup dry bread crumbs	1 cup milk
¼ cup chopped celery	½ tsp salt
3 tbsp chopped onion	½ tsp prepared mustard
1 cup cooked rice	2 tbsp melted butter

Pour into greased loaf pan lined with waxed paper. Place loaf pan in shallow pan half full of boiling water. Bake at 325° for 1 hour. Serves 6.

CRUSTY MEAT LOAF

Mix

1½ lbs hamburger	½ cup water
1 egg, slightly beaten	2 tbsp chopped onion
½ cup bread crumbs	1½ tsp salt
½ cup catsup	

Form into loaf and gently press 1½ cups buttered bread cubes into top of loaf. Bake at 350° for 1 hour. Serves 6.

COUNTRY STUFFED MEAT LOAF

Sauté 1 cup chopped onions and 1 cup chopped celery in ¼ cup hot fat.

Add

  ⅓ cup chopped green pepper   ½ cup water
  2 eggs, slightly beaten   1 tbsp salt
  3 cups dry bread crumbs

Mix and add half of this stuffing to 2 lbs hamburger. Put half of this mixture in a greased loaf pan. Cover with remaining stuffing and top with balance of meat mixture. Bake at 350° for 75 minutes. Baste at 15-minute intervals with a mixture of ½ cup tomato juice and 2 tbsp melted butter. Serves 10.

VARIATION: Slice cold in ½-inch slices. Place slices in a pan and cover with condensed beef bouillon. Cover and heat at 350° for 35 minutes.

COUNTRY STUFFED MEAT ROLL

Mix 1½ lbs hamburger with 1 tsp salt and ¼ tsp pepper.
Shape meat into a 10 x 12-inch rectangle on waxed paper. Set aside and mix stuffing.

Mix

  1½ cups whole-kernel corn   2 tbsp chopped parsley
  1 cup bread crumbs   ½ tsp salt
  1 egg, slightly beaten   ⅛ tsp pepper
  ¼ cup chopped onion

Mix well, top meat rectangle with stuffing, roll like a jelly roll, bake at 350° for 1 hour. Serves 8.

DAIRY MEAT LOAF

Mix

1 lb hamburger	½ cup cottage cheese
1 cup bread crumbs	½ cup sour cream
1 cup grated carrots	1 tsp Worcestershire sauce
½ tsp salt	¼ tsp marjoram
½ cup chopped onions	

Shape into loaf. Bake at 350° for 1 hour. Serves 6.

DIETETIC MEAT LOAF

Soften 2 slices well-browned toast in ½ cup non-fat skimmed milk.

Add

1 lb lean hamburger	¾ tsp salt
1 egg, slightly beaten	¼ tsp pepper
⅓ cup minced onion	

Form into a loaf and place in the center of a baking dish. Top with ½ cup chili sauce and pour ½ cup condensed beef bouillon around loaf. Bake at 350° for 1½ hours. Serves 4.

EASY MEAT LOAF

Mix

1 lb hamburger	1 tsp salt
1 cup grated raw potatoes	¼ tsp pepper
½ cup grated raw carrots	½ tsp onion salt
2 eggs, slightly beaten	

Form into loaf and bake at 375° for 1 hour. Serves 4.

FATHER'S MEAT LOAF

Mix

2 lbs hamburger	2 tbsp horseradish
2 eggs, slightly beaten	2 tsp salt
2 cups bread crumbs	⅛ tsp pepper
1 cup chopped onion	1 tsp dry mustard
½ cup chopped green pepper	¼ cup catsup
¼ cup milk	

Shape into loaf and brush ¼ cup catsup over top. Bake at 350° for 1 hour. Spoon juices over top when serving. Serves 8.

GLAZED MEAT LOAF

Mix

1½ lbs hamburger	2 tbsp catsup
¾ cup soft bread crumbs	½ tsp dry mustard
¾ cup milk	2 eggs, slightly beaten
¾ cup chopped onion	1½ tsp salt
¼ cup chopped green pepper	¼ tsp pepper
2 tsp Worcestershire sauce	

Shape into loaf. Beat ⅔ cup currant jelly and stir in 3 tbsp prepared mustard. Bake loaf at 350° for 45 minutes. Spread jelly over top and bake 20 minutes more. Serves 6.

DILL MEAT LOAVES

Fry 4 slices bacon crisp and sauté 1 cup onions in 2 tbsp bacon fat. Put aside.

Mix

1 lb hamburger	1 tsp dry mustard
¼ cup dry bread crumbs	1 tsp Worcestershire sauce
¼ cup tomato juice	1 tsp salt
1 egg, slightly beaten	⅛ tsp pepper

Pat out meat mixture in 4 layers on flour-covered waxed paper. Place a strip of dill pickle on each layer. Spread crumbled bacon and onions over layers. Roll up as for jelly rolls. Bake rolls at 350° for 35 minutes. Serves 4.

HAMBURGER AND SAUSAGE LOAF

Mix

1½ lbs hamburger	½ cup milk
½ lb sausage	½ tsp nutmeg
1 cup chopped onion	½ tsp allspice
1 egg, slightly beaten	1 tsp salt
1 cup bread crumbs	¼ tsp pepper

Shape into loaf. Bake at 350° for 1¼ hours. Serves 8.

HAMBURGER IN A BLANKET

Mix

1½ lbs hamburger	1¼ tsp salt
1 egg, slightly beaten	⅛ tsp pepper
½ cup chili sauce	½ tsp monosodium
1 tbsp Worcestershire sauce	glutamate
¼ cup water	

Shape into a roll and set aside.

Add 1 tbsp chopped onion and ¼ cup chopped parsley to 2 cups packaged biscuit mix and follow directions on package. Roll dough into a 12-inch square. Roll up meat roll in dough,

sealing all edges. Bake, seam side down, in a baking dish at 400°
for 45 minutes, or until crust is done. Serves 8.

HAMBURGER LUNCHEON MEAT LOAF

Mix

1 lb hamburger	½ cup pineapple juice
1 12-oz can ground luncheon	2 tbsp quick-cooking tapioca
meat	1¼ tsp salt
½ cup crushed pineapple	

Shape into loaf and place in a baking dish.

Mix until dissolved

½ cup brown sugar	¼ cup vinegar
½ tsp dry mustard	¼ cup water

Pour over meat loaf and bake at 350° for 1 hour. Baste every
10 minutes. Serves 8.

HAMBURGER VEGETABLE ROLL

Mix

1 lb hamburger	2 tbsp cooking oil
1 egg, slightly beaten	½ cup bread crumbs
2 tbsp milk	¼ tsp pepper
1 tsp salt	

Form mixture into square ½ inch thick on waxed paper.
Spread 1½ cups seasoned mashed potatoes on half of the square.
Spread 1½ cups seasoned mashed peas on other ½ of square.
Start with potato end and roll like a jelly roll. Wrap with waxed
paper and chill in refrigerator. When chilled, cut into 1-inch
slices and place on broiler rack 4 inches from heat source. Brush
with oil. Broil 10 minutes. Turn, brush with oil, and broil 10 more
minutes. Serves 6.

HAMBURGER FRUIT ROLL

Mix

1½ lbs hamburger	1 tsp salt
½ lb ground lean pork	¼ tsp pepper
1 egg, slightly beaten	½ tsp marjoram

On waxed paper, roll out to a square ½ inch thick.

Mix

4 cups toasted bread cubes	½ cup sour cream
½ cup seedless raisins	1 tsp salt
⅓ cup chopped onion	¼ tsp pepper
1 cup cottage cheese	

Spread on meat mixture to within ¼ inch of edges. Roll up like a jelly roll and place in baking dish. Arrange 10 half rings of pineapple around roll and bake at 350° for 1 hour. Serves 8 to 10.

HAMBURGER HAM LOAF

Mix

1 lb hamburger	1½ cups cracker crumbs
1 lb sausage	2 cups tomatoes
½ lb ground smoked ham	½ tsp salt
2 eggs, slightly beaten	

Shape into loaf. Bake at 350° for 2 hours. Serves 8.

VARIATION: Serve with horseradish sauce, as follows:

½ cup mayonnaise	⅛ tsp salt
2 tbsp catsup	¼ cup chopped sweet pickles
3 tbsp horseradish	

Mix and chill.

HAMBURGER RING

Combine 1 lb hamburger with ½ lb ground pork.

Add

2 tbsp chopped onion	¾ cup milk
¼ cup chopped green pepper	1 tsp prepared mustard
1 beaten egg	2 tbsp prepared horseradish
1 cup wheat germ	1 tsp salt

Mix well. Pack into greased 1½-qt ring mold; place in pan of hot water. Bake at 375° for 1¼ hours. Unmold, brown under broiler for 5–10 minutes. Serves 6.

IOWA MEAT LOAF

Mix

1 lb hamburger	⅔ cup evaporated milk
½ cup chopped onion	½ cup cracker crumbs
¼ cup chopped green pepper	1 tsp salt
1 egg, slightly beaten	

Form into 2-inch rolls, brown on all sides in hot fat, bake in casserole at 350° for 40 minutes. Serves 4.

ISLAND MEAT LOAF

Mix

1 lb hamburger	⅔ cup crushed pineapple
½ lb ground pork	½ cup pineapple juice
½ lb ground veal	½ tsp marjoram
1½ cups bread crumbs	1 tsp dry mustard
2 eggs, slightly beaten	2 tsp salt
2 tbsp chopped pimiento	¼ tsp pepper

Shape into loaf and bake at 350° for 50 minutes. Place strips of bacon and pineapple chunks on top of loaf and bake for 20 minutes more. Serves 8.

LITTLE PIG MEAT LOAF

Mix

2 lbs hamburger	2 tbsp catsup
1 cup soft bread crumbs	1 tsp dry mustard
1 cup milk	2 eggs, slightly beaten
1 cup chopped onion	2 tsp salt
½ cup chopped green pepper	½ tsp pepper
1 tbsp Worcestershire sauce	

Shape into loaf. Press 8 small pork sausages into top of loaf. Bake at 350° for 1 hour. Serves 8.

MEAT LOAF SOMERSET

Mix

1 lb hamburger	2 tbsp minced celery
½ lb ground pork	2 eggs, slightly beaten
½ lb ground veal	1 cup tomatoes
1 cup cracker crumbs	1 tsp salt
2 tbsp chopped parsley	¼ tsp paprika
1 tbsp minced green pepper	

Pack lightly into loaf pan. Bake at 350° for 40 minutes.

Sauce:

⅓ cup brown sugar	⅓ tsp cinnamon
⅓ cup crushed pineapple	2 tbsp butter

Mix and spread over the hot loaf. Bake at 350° for 20 minutes. Serves 8.

LITTLE WHEAT LOAVES

Mix

¾ lb hamburger	2 tbsp chopped parsley
½ lb ground pork	½ tsp crushed bay leaf
¼ lb ground beef liver	½ tsp ground thyme
2 eggs, slightly beaten	¾ cup crushed wheat flakes
¾ cup chopped onion	⅛ tsp pepper

Shape into 8 little loaves about 3 inches long and roll in 1½ cups uncrushed whole wheat flakes. Bake in shallow pan at 350° for 35 minutes. Serves 8.

MACARONI AND CHEESE MEAT LOAF

Cook 4 oz macaroni according to directions on package.

Mix

cooked macaroni	2 tbsp chopped green pepper
1 lb hamburger	⅓ cup grated Cheddar
½ cup soft bread crumbs	cheese
½ cup milk	1 tsp salt
2 eggs, slightly beaten	¼ tsp pepper
½ cup chopped onion	

Shape loaf. Bake at 350° for 1 hour. Serves 6.

MEAT LOAF FOR TWENTY-FOUR

Mix

6 lbs hamburger	4 cups evaporated milk
2 cups chopped green pepper	3 cups bread crumbs
2 cups chopped onion	6 tsp salt
6 slightly beaten eggs	1½ tsp pepper

Shape into 3 loaves and bake at 350° for 40 minutes. Serves 24.

MEAT ROLL NAPOLI

Mix

1 lb hamburger	3 tbsp minced parsley
½ cup soft bread crumbs	1 tsp salt
½ cup milk	¼ tsp pepper
2 eggs, slightly beaten	4 tbsp Parmesan cheese
2 minced cloves garlic	

Pat out meat mixture on floured waxed paper. Place 6 thin slices ham and 6 thin slices provolone cheese on layer. Roll as for jelly roll. Bake at 350° for 45 minutes. Serves 4.

MUSHROOM-STUFFED MEAT LOAF

Mix

3 lbs hamburger	1 tbsp salt
2 eggs, slightly beaten	¼ tsp pepper
¼ cup milk	½ tsp monosodium
⅓ cup catsup	glutamate
1½ tsp dry mustard	

Put aside and in ¼ cup butter sauté the following for 4 minutes:

1 lb sliced mushrooms (save out 8 whole)	¾ cup chopped onion
	1 tsp lemon juice

Mix in

4 cups bread crumbs	¼ tsp thyme
1 tsp salt	½ tsp monosodium
⅛ tsp pepper	glutamate
¼ cup minced parsley	

Press ½ of meat mixture into a loaf pan, cover with stuffing, and top with rest of meat mixture. Push 8 whole mushrooms into top and refrigerate for 1½ hours. Bake at 400° for 1 hour and 10 minutes. Serves 10.

VARIATION: To glaze, brush top with heated currant jelly.

MERINGUE MEAT LOAF

Mix

1½ lbs hamburger
1½ cups bread crumbs
⅓ cup finely chopped green pepper
4 egg yolks, slightly beaten

⅓ cup catsup
2 tbsp prepared mustard
½ cup minced onion
2 tbsp horseradish

Form into a loaf and bake at 325° for 30 minutes.

Beat 4 egg whites well. Add ¼ tsp cream of tartar and beat until very stiff. Fold in 4 tbsp prepared mustard and spread on top of hot meat loaf. Bake 25 minutes more. Serves 6.

MOTHER'S MEAT LOAF

Mix

1 lb hamburger
⅓ cup chopped onion
1 8-oz can tomato sauce
1 egg, slightly beaten

1 cup cracker crumbs
1 tsp salt
¼ tsp pepper

Shape into loaf. Bake at 350° for 1 hour. Serves 4.

MUSHROOM MEAT LOAF

Sauté 3 cups chopped mushrooms and ½ cup chopped onions in 3 tbsp butter over a low heat until brown, about 15 minutes. Combine mushrooms and onions with

1 lb hamburger
½ cup bread crumbs
1 egg, slightly beaten
1 tbsp chopped pimiento
⅔ cup cream

2 tbsp chopped parsley
½ tsp paprika
1 tsp salt
¼ tsp pepper

Shape into loaf, press sliced mushrooms into top of loaf, and bake at 350° for 1 hour. Serves 4.

NEW-POTATO MEAT RING

Mix

1 lb hamburger
¼ lb ground pork
¼ lb ground smoked ham
2 cups grated raw potatoes
2 eggs, slightly beaten

½ cup chopped onion
1 tsp salt
½ tsp thyme
½ tsp rosemary

Bake in greased 8-inch ring mold at 350° for 1 hour. Unmold on serving platter. Fill center of ring with creamed new potatoes. Serves 6.

NORWEGIAN MEAT LOAF AND GRAVY

Mix

2 lbs hamburger
2 eggs, slightly beaten
¾ cup flour
1 cup milk

1 tsp salt
¼ tsp pepper
1 tsp nutmeg

Shape into loaf and set aside.

Sauté 1 cup chopped onions in 3 tbsp cooking oil. Combine with 2 cans condensed beef bouillon and 2 cups of water and bring to boil. Tie meat loaf in cheesecloth and place in broth. Simmer for 35 minutes. Remove meat loaf and strain broth. To make gravy, add 1 cup milk mixed with ⅓ cup flour to strained broth and bring to a boil. Season with 2 tbsp steak sauce. Serves 8.

OLD-FASHIONED MEAT LOAF

Mix

1 lb hamburger	¼ cup chopped green pepper
½ lb ground pork	2 tbsp horseradish
½ lb ground veal	1 tbsp salt
2 eggs, slightly beaten	¼ cup milk
2 cups soft bread crumbs	¼ cup catsup
¾ cup chopped onion	1 tsp dry mustard

Shape loaf. Bake at 400° for 70 minutes. Serves 6.

POT-ROASTED MEAT LOAF AND VEGETABLES

Mix

1 lb hamburger	1 tsp salt
¼ lb ground pork	¼ tsp pepper
1 egg, slightly beaten	½ cup water
2 tbsp flour	

Shape into flat loaf, dust with flour, brown on both sides in 2 tbsp hot drippings in large heavy kettle. Remove loaf from kettle.

Place in kettle

8 carrots	2 white diced turnips
8 medium onions	4 sliced stalks celery
2 sliced parsnips	¼ tsp pepper
1 tsp salt	

Stir until mixed. Add 1 8-oz can tomato sauce. Place loaf on top of vegetables and sauce. Cover and cook over low heat for 1 hour. Do not add more water. Serves 6.

OLIVE MEAT LOAF

Mix

1 lb hamburger	1 cup cottage cheese
1 lb ground lean pork	1 egg, slightly beaten
1½ cups chopped olives	½ tsp salt
2 cups soft bread crumbs	¼ tsp pepper

Bake in greased loaf pan at 350° for 1 hour. Serves 8.

ONION SOUP MEAT LOAF

Mix

2 lbs hamburger	1 cup hot water
½ pkg dehydrated onion soup	2 tsp salt
	¼ tsp pepper
1 egg, slightly beaten	½ tsp monosodium
16 crushed crackers	glutamate

Shape into a loaf pan and bake at 350° for 1 hour and 15 minutes. Serves 8.

PATIO MEAT LOAF FOR FIFTY

Mix

11 lbs hamburger	4 qts bread crumbs
3 cups chopped onion	3 cups tomato juice
3 cups chopped green pepper	2½ cups water
4 cups chopped celery	4 tbsp salt
2 cups melted butter	2 tsp pepper
10 eggs, slightly beaten	

Form into 6 loaves and bake at 350° for 1 hour. Serves 50.

ONION RING MEAT LOAF

Thinly slice one onion into baking dish. Mix 1½ tsp salt with 1½ lbs hamburger and form into loaf. Place on onion rings. Top loaf with 6 more onion rings and pour 1 can condensed tomato soup over all. Sprinkle with ⅛ tsp oregano and ½ tsp basil. Bake at 350° for 1 hour. Serves 6.

PINEAPPLE MEAT LOAF

Mix

2 lbs hamburger	¾ cup crushed pineapple
1 beaten egg	and juice
1 chopped pimiento	1 cup bread crumbs
2 tsp salt	

Place 3 slices bacon in bottom of loaf pan. Shape meat mixture on bacon. Place 3 more slices bacon on top of meat loaf. Bake at 350° for 1½ hours. Serves 8.

POTATO-FROSTED MEAT LOAF

Mix

1 lb hamburger	1 tbsp catsup
½ cup milk	½ tsp dry mustard
½ cup soft bread crumbs	1 egg, slightly beaten
½ cup chopped onion	2 tbsp chopped green pepper
1 tsp salt	½ tbsp Worcestershire sauce
¼ tsp pepper	1 8-oz can tomato sauce

Shape loaf. Bake at 350° for 40 minutes. Remove from oven. Add 2 tbsp chopped green onion to 1½ cups well-seasoned mashed potatoes and frost top of loaf. Bake at 350° for 20 minutes. Serves 4.

POTATO MEAT ROLL

Mix

1¼ lb hamburger	1½ tsp salt
1 egg, slightly beaten	¼ tsp pepper
½ lb ground smoked ham	½ cup chopped onion
½ cup bread crumbs	

Set aside. Mix

1 egg, slightly beaten	⅛ tsp pepper
½ can condensed mushroom soup	2 cups unseasoned mashed potatoes
1 tsp salt	

Shape meat mixture into 10 x 14-inch rectangle on waxed paper. Place potato mixture diagonally across meat rectangle. Roll like a jelly roll and bake seam side down at 350° for 1¼ hours. Serves 8.

POTTED MEAT LOAVES

Mix

1 lb hamburger	½ 8-oz can tomato sauce
½ cup chopped onion	1 tbsp Worcestershire sauce
1 egg, slightly beaten	2 tbsp chopped green pepper
½ cup bread crumbs	½ tsp dry mustard
½ cup milk	1 tsp salt
2 tbsp catsup	¼ tsp pepper

Shape into 4 loaves and dust with flour on both sides. Brown loaves on all sides and remove from skillet. In same skillet add

1½ cups sliced onions	½ tsp salt
2 tbsp chopped parsley	⅛ tsp pepper

Put loaves on top of onions and add 1 cup condensed beef bouillon. Cover and cook slowly for 30 minutes. Serves 4.

QUICK MEAT LOAF FOR TWELVE

Mix

2½ lbs hamburger	1 can condensed tomato
1 lb ground veal	soup
½ lb ground lean pork	1 can condensed bean soup
2 cups soft bread crumbs	4 tsp salt
1 cup finely chopped onions	1 tsp pepper
4 eggs, slightly beaten	

Pack into a greased loaf pan and bake at 350° for 1¼ hours. Serves 12.

RICE LAYER LOAF

Mix

1¾ lbs hamburger	¼ cup chopped parsley
1 lb ground pork	¼ tsp thyme
2 cups soft bread crumbs	2 tsp salt
1 cup milk	¼ tsp pepper
1 egg, slightly beaten	1 tbsp brown sugar
1 tsp Worcestershire sauce	1 tbsp wine vinegar
½ cup chopped onion	

Prepare 1⅓ cups minute-type precooked rice according to directions on package, adding

1 tbsp chopped onion	½ tsp monosodium
½ tsp salt	glutamate
Dash of pepper	

When rice is done, mix in 1 tbsp chopped parsley and 1 slightly beaten egg. Spread ⅓ of meat mixture into greased loaf pan. Top with half of rice mixture. Repeat layers and top with meat mixture. Bake at 350° for 1½ hours. Serves 8.

RED CAP MEAT LOAVES

Mix

1½ lbs hamburger	1 egg, slightly beaten
½ cup soft bread crumbs	1 tbsp Worcestershire sauce
½ cup chili sauce	½ tsp salt

Shape 3 tbsp of meat mixture around bottom and sides of 6 large muffin tins. Mix ¾ cup shredded sharp American cheese with ½ cup of chopped black olives and put 2 tbsp in each cup. Make 6 patties 1 inch thick and place over each cup. Seal and bake at 350° for 20 minutes. Put tomato slice on top of each and bake 10 minutes. Serves 6.

SHERRY MEAT LOAVES

Mix

1½ lbs hamburger	½ 8-oz can tomato sauce
1 egg, slightly beaten	1½ tsp salt
1 cup bread crumbs	¼ tsp pepper
3 tbsp chopped onion	

Shape into 4 individual meat loaves and bake in shallow dish at 350° for 40 minutes.

Combine 1 tbsp cornstarch with 2 tbsp brown sugar and stir in

1 beef bouillon cube dissolved in ¾ cup hot water	¾ cup sherry
	1 tbsp vinegar
½ 8-oz can tomato sauce	1 tsp prepared mustard

Cook, stirring until thick. Drain juice off meat loaves and pour sauce over loaves. Bake 30 minutes longer, basting every 5 minutes. Serves 4.

RICE MEAT LOAF

Mix

1 lb hamburger	½ tsp thyme
1 egg, slightly beaten	1 tsp salt
½ cup milk	⅛ tsp pepper
¼ cup minced onion	1 cup cooked rice

Shape into a loaf. Bake in greased pan at 350° for 45 minutes. Serves 6.

VARIATION: Serve with creamed tomato sauce, as follows:

1 8-oz can tomato sauce	½ tsp salt
1 3-oz can diced mushrooms	⅛ tsp pepper

Mix all ingredients and heat. Add 1 cup sour cream and reheat, stirring constantly.

SPANISH MEAT LOAF

Soak 1½ cups diced bread in ½ cup milk. Mash until broken up.

Mix with

1½ lbs hamburger	2 tbsp chopped onion
½ lb ground pork	2 tsp salt
1 egg, slightly beaten	¼ tsp pepper

Form into loaf.

Sauce:

2 cups canned tomatoes	2 tbsp sugar
¼ cup onions, chopped fine	2 tbsp flour

Mix and spread over top of loaf. Bake at 350° for 1¼ hours. Serves 6 to 8.

SAVORY MEAT LOAF

Mix

2 lbs hamburger	1 cup thick cream sauce
½ lb ground pork	1 tsp sugar
1 cup chopped onion	2 tsp salt
1 cup dry bread crumbs	¼ tsp pepper
1½ cups canned tomatoes	

Shape and put in loaf pan. Lay 2 strips bacon on top. Bake at 350° for 1 hour. Serves 8.

SNOW-CAPPED MEAT LOAF

Mix

1 lb hamburger	¾ cup chopped onion
½ cup uncooked oatmeal	1 tsp salt
⅔ cup sour cream	½ tsp pepper
1 egg, slightly beaten	

Place into greased loaf pan. Mix 1 cup cottage cheese with ½ cup mashed potatoes and spread evenly over loaf. Bake at 325° for 50 minutes. Serves 4 to 6.

SUNSHINE MEAT LOAF

Mix

1 lb hamburger	½ cup chopped onion
½ lb ground pork	1 egg, slightly beaten
½ cup milk	1 tsp salt
½ cup bread crumbs	¼ tsp thyme

Shape loaf and press 6 peach halves into top of loaf. Put 1 tsp catsup in hollow of each peach. Bake at 350° for 1 hour. Serves 6.

SOUR CREAM STUFFED MEAT LOAF

Mix

1 lb hamburger	1 tbsp chopped parsley
½ cup sour cream	½ tsp salt
¼ cup chopped green pepper	¼ tsp pepper

To make stuffing, sauté ½ cup chopped onion and ½ cup chopped celery until soft.

Add

1½ cups bread crumbs	2 tbsp melted butter
½ cup sour cream	⅛ tsp rosemary
1 egg, slightly beaten	½ tsp salt
¼ cup chicken stock	

Mix a third of this mixture with the meat mixture, then put half of this meat mixture in the bottom of a baking pan, spread stuffing over meat, and top with remaining meat mixture. Bake at 350° for 45 minutes. Serves 4.

SPICY MEAT LOAF

Mix

1 lb hamburger	¼ tsp fennel seed
½ cup bread crumbs	1 tsp salt
½ cup milk	¼ tsp pepper
¼ cup grated onion	½ tsp paprika
1 egg, slightly beaten	¼ tsp oregano
2 tbsp chopped parsley	¼ tsp basil
1 clove chopped garlic	

Shape into loaf and bake at 350° for 1 hour. Serve cold, sliced very thin. Serves 4.

STUFFED MEAT LOAF

Mix

½ cup wheat germ	1 tsp grated onion
½ cup tomato juice	¼ cup chopped green pepper
2 lbs hamburger	

Stuffing:

Sauté 4 cups dried bread cubes in 4 tbsp melted butter until lightly browned. Remove from heat.

Add

½ cup wheat germ	½ cup tomato juice
½ cup celery, finely chopped	1 egg, slightly beaten
¼ cup grated onion	

Divided meat mixture in half, place one half in greased loaf pan. Spread stuffing over meat. Place remaining meat over stuffing. Shape into round loaf. Bake at 350° for 1 hour. Serves 8.

VEGETABLE SOUP MEAT LOAF

Mix

1 lb hamburger	½ cup bread crumbs
1 can condensed vegetable soup	1 tsp salt
½ cup chopped onion	½ tsp monosodium glutamate

Spoon into 12 2-inch cupcake tins and bake at 450° for 15 minutes. Serves 6.

SWEET 'N' SOUR MEAT LOAF

Mix

1 8-oz can tomato sauce	¼ cup vinegar
¼ cup brown sugar	1 tsp prepared mustard

Mix

1 egg, slightly beaten with fork	2 lbs hamburger
	1½ tsp salt
¼ cup minced onion	¼ tsp black pepper
¼ cup crushed crackers	½ cup tomato sauce mixture

Shape meat into oval loaf. Place in shallow baking dish. Pour rest of tomato sauce mixture on top. Bake at 400° for 45 minutes. Serves 8.

SWEET PICKLE-STUFFED MEAT LOAF

Mix

1 lb hamburger	½ cup milk
¾ cup bread crumbs	1 tsp Worcestershire sauce
2 eggs, slightly beaten	¼ tsp basil
4 tbsp chili sauce	1 tsp salt
2 tbsp chopped green pepper	¼ tsp pepper

To make stuffing, sauté ½ cup chopped onions and ¼ cup chopped celery in 3 tbsp butter until soft. Combine with

½ cup chopped sweet pickles	¼ tsp marjoram
1½ cups bread crumbs	½ tsp salt
⅓ cup chopped pimientos	⅛ tsp pepper

Press half of meat mixture into a loaf pan, spread stuffing on meat, and top with other half of meat mixture. Bake at 350° for 1 hour. Serves 4 to 6.

VARIATION: English Walnut Stuffing:

Sauté ¾ cup chopped onions and ¼ cup chopped celery in 3 tbsp butter until soft.

Combine with

1 cup chopped English walnuts	2 tbsp sugar
1½ cups bread crumbs	1 tbsp brown sugar
⅓ cup milk	½ tsp salt
2 eggs, slightly beaten	½ tsp monosodium glutamate

Mix well and follow baking instructions above.

MAIN DISHES

HAMBURGER AVOCADO

Season 1 lb hamburger with 1 tsp salt and brown in a skillet with 1 tbsp cooking oil. When brown, add 1 crushed avocado, stir and serve. The kids love this one. Serves 4.

HAMBURGER BIRDS

Mix

1 lb hamburger	1 green pepper, chopped fine
1 cup fine bread crumbs	2 tbsp chopped stuffed olives
½ cup milk	2 tbsp chopped pimiento
Juice of 1 lemon	1 tsp salt
½ cup grated American cheese	

Form into 6 rolls, wrap a strip of bacon around each roll, and sear in deep fat. Put in a covered baking dish with ¼ cup water and bake at 350° for 1 hour. Serves 6.

HAMBURGER CHILI FOR TWENTY-FOUR

Sauté 3 cloves minced garlic and 3 pints chopped onion in ¾ cup cooking oil. Brown 6 lbs hamburger until crumbled, put all in a large kettle.

Add

6 No. 2½ cans tomatoes	1 tsp cuminseed
6 No. 303 cans red kidney	2 tbsp salt
beans	1½ tsp pepper
2 tsp chili powder	

Cover and simmer for 1½ hours. Serves 24.

HAMBURGER CHOP SUEY

In a large skillet, sauté ¾ lb hamburger, ¾ cup sliced onion, and 1 cup celery strips in 2 tbsp cooking oil until lightly browned. Add 1 No. 303 can drained bean sprouts, 1 can condensed beef bouillon, and 1 2-oz can drained, sliced mushrooms (save liquid). Mix 1 tbsp cornstarch with mushroom liquid until smooth and add to the mixture. Cook for 10 minutes, stirring constantly. Add ⅓ cup soy sauce. Serve over cooked rice. Serves 6.

HAMBURGER CREOLE

In 3 tbsp bacon fat, sauté ¼ cup chopped onions. Brown 1 lb hamburger.

Add

½ cup diced celery	3 tbsp flour
¼ cup chopped green pepper	2 cups canned tomatoes
1 tbsp minced parsley	1 tsp salt

Simmer for 15 minutes until thick and creamy. Serves 4.

HAMBURGER DELMONICO STEAK

Mix

1 lb hamburger	1 tsp salt
½ cup milk	⅓ tsp black pepper

Form into a large flat steak about 1½ inches thick. Broil on both sides 3 inches from heat source until desired rareness. Serve topped with fried onions. Serves 2.

HAMBURGER GUMBO

Brown 1 lb hamburger and ¾ cup chopped onion until hamburger is crumbly and onion is soft.

Add

1 can condensed chicken gumbo soup	1 tsp salt
	¼ tsp pepper
2 tbsp catsup	¼ tsp monosodium
2 tbsp prepared mustard	glutamate

Simmer over a low heat for 30 minutes. Serve over split toasted buns. Serves 6.

HAMBURGER MEXICAN RICE

Cut 3 slices bacon into pieces. Fry, add 1½ cups chopped onions, 1 cup chopped green pepper, and 1 lb hamburger. Cook for about 5 minutes.

Add

3 cups canned tomatoes	1½ tsp salt
½ cup uncooked rice	¼ tsp pepper
1 tsp chili powder	

Simmer for about 1 hour, or until rice is cooked. If mixture cooks down too much, add a little water. Serves 4.

HAMBURGER MEAT ROLL

In 2 tbsp cooking fat, brown ¼ cup minced onion, 1 minced clove garlic, ½ lb hamburger, and 1 tsp bottled meat sauce.

Add

1 6-oz can tomato paste	1 tsp salt
½ cup diced green pepper	⅛ tsp pepper
2 tsp sugar	⅛ tsp powdered oregano
¼ tsp chili powder	

Simmer for about 10 minutes and cool slightly. In the meantime, prepare 1 cup biscuit mix according to directions on package and roll out to a rectangle about 8 x 12 inches. Spread meat mixture almost to edges of dough, roll like a jelly roll, and place in a greased baking pan. Bake at 375° for 25 minutes. Serves 4.

HAMBURGER AND NOODLES IN SOUR CREAM

In 2 tbsp cooking fat, brown 1 lb hamburger and 1 cup chopped onion. Place 3 cups uncooked noodles over meat.

Add

3 cups tomato juice	1½ tsp salt
2 tsp Worcestershire sauce	¼ tsp pepper
2 tsp celery salt	

Cover and simmer for 30 minutes. Stir in 1 cup sour cream, bring to boil, and serve. Serves 6.

HAMBURGER AND NOODLE CAKE

Brown ¾ lb hamburger and ¼ cup minced onion in 1 tbsp cooking fat until hamburger looses its red color. Cook 1 8-oz package noodles according to directions on package. Mix the meat and noodles and fry in a skillet with 4 tbsp butter until brown on the underside. Turn out on a plate and melt 1 tbsp butter in skillet. Return cake to skillet to brown second side. Sprinkle with grated Cheddar and cut in wedges. Serves 6.

HAMBURGER ONION PIE

Prepare biscuit mix according to directions on package and roll into a circle to fit a 9-inch piepan. Sauté 1½ cups sliced onions and 1 lb hamburger until meat loses its red color. Add 1 tsp salt, ¼ tsp pepper, and ½ tsp monosodium glutamate. Spread on the dough in pie tin. Beat 2 eggs lightly and mix with 1 cup cottage cheese. Pour over meat and sprinkle with paprika. Bake at 375° for 30 minutes. Serves 6.

HAMBURGER ONION SATELLITES

Sauté ¼ lb fresh sliced mushrooms in 2 tbsp butter. Remove from pan. Do not rinse pan. In same pan, brown ½ lb hamburger and ½ lb bulk pork sausage. Remove from pan and, while pan is still very hot, pour in 1 pint chicken stock. When stock is hot, add 2 lbs peeled little pearl onions. Cover and simmer for about 30 minutes, or until onions are tender. Add mushrooms and meat and mix well. Just before serving, blend in 1 8-oz carton sour cream and top with chopped pistachio nuts. Serves 6.

HAMBURGER PATTIES

Mix 1 lb hamburger, 1 tsp salt, and ¼ tsp pepper. Shape into 4 patties and broil or grill to desired rareness. Top with one of the following combinations:

1. 2 tbsp melted butter, 2 tbsp chili sauce, 1 tsp prepared mustard, and dash of chili powder.

2. 2 tbsp melted butter, 3 tbsp catsup, and dash of black pepper.

3. 2 tbsp melted butter and 3 tbsp chopped chives.

4. 2 tbsp melted butter and 3 tbsp crumbled blue cheese.

5. 2 tbsp melted butter, ½ cup water, ¼ package onion soup mix, and 1 tsp flour. Heat and pour over patties.

6. 3 tbsp melted butter, 2 tbsp lemon juice, ½ tsp salt, 1 tsp dry mustard, ½ tsp paprika, 2 tsp water, and dash of Louisiana hot sauce.

7. 2 tbsp melted butter, 1 can condensed cream of mushroom soup, ¼ cup sherry, ½ cup canned mushrooms, and ¼ cup grated sharp cheese. Heat and pour over patties.

8. ½ package chive cheese, melted, ¼ cup milk, and ⅛ tsp black pepper.

9. 2 tbsp melted butter, 1 tbsp Worcestershire sauce, ¼ cup chili sauce, and ½ cup grated Cheddar cheese.

10. Add 2 tbsp butter to drippings in pan and pour over patties.

11. 2 large sliced onions, sautéed in drippings.

12. Cook 1½ cups sliced onions in boiling water until soft. Drain and save water. Press onions through a sieve. Melt 3 tbsp butter in a saucepan, blend in 3 tbsp flour, and add 1 cup of the onion liquor, ½ cup milk, ½ tsp salt, and ⅛ tsp black pepper. Cook, stirring constantly, until smooth. Add the onion pulp and reheat. Pour over patties.

13. Melt 2 tbsp butter in a saucepan. Blend in 2 tbsp flour. Mix ½ cup condensed beef bouillon and ½ cup cream and add to butter mixture. Cook over a low heat, stirring constantly, until smooth and thick. Mix 2 tsp dry mustard in ½ cup water and stir into sauce. Stir a little of the hot sauce into 1 beaten egg yolk. Add egg mixture quickly to hot sauce in pan. Cook and stir until mixture is hot.

BARBECUED HAMBURGER PATTIES

Mix

1½ lbs hamburger	1 tsp salt
½ cup bread crumbs in ¾ cup milk	¼ tsp pepper

Form into 6 patties and brown on both sides in skillet with 2 tbsp cooking fat. Melt 2 tbsp butter in a saucepan and add ¼ cup chopped onion and ¼ cup chopped celery. Stir and cook until onion is yellow, then add

½ cup tomato paste	2 tbsp sugar
2 tbsp vinegar	¼ tsp Tabasco

Pour sauce over patties and cook until meat is done, basting sauce over meat as it cooks. Serves 6.

MARINATED HAMBURGER PATTIES

Mix

1 lb hamburger	¼ tsp pepper
3 tbsp chopped onion	½ tsp monosodium
1 tsp salt	glutamate

Form into 6 patties. Marinate patties in 1 cup French dressing in a shallow dish for 45 minutes. Pan-broil over a medium heat for 5 minutes on each side or until desired rareness. Mix 1 can chunk pineapple with juices in pan and serve over patties. Serves 6.

DIETETIC HAMBURGER PATTIES

Form lean hamburger into thick patties. Sprinkle salt in the bottom of an iron skillet and heat. Place patties in skillet and brown bottoms. Remove from skillet and make a depression in tops of patties. Fill depression with Worcestershire sauce and brown tops in a broiler 3 inches from heat source until desired rareness.

HAMBURGER PATTIES IN LEMON SAUCE

Mix

1 lb hamburger	¼ tsp pepper
2 tbsp minced onion	½ tsp monosodium
½ cup chopped walnuts	glutamate
1 tsp salt	

Form into 6 patties and brown on both sides in a skillet with 3 tbsp cooking fat. Remove from skillet and sauté 1 large onion (cut into rings) until tender and golden in color. Remove onion rings, and in same skillet mix

1 can condensed beef bouillon	1 crushed bay leaf
⅔ cup fresh lemon juice	1 tsp dry mustard
⅓ cup brown sugar	½ tsp salt
2 tbsp cornstarch in 4 tbsp water	¼ tsp pepper

Simmer until sauce is slightly thickened, then add hamburger patties and top with onion rings and lemon slices. Cover and cook for about 35 minutes. Serves 6.

HAMBURGER ROLLS

Mix ½ lb hamburger with ¾ lb sausage and form into 32 small rolls. Prepare hot-roll mix according to directions on package and let it rise once. Turn out on a flat, lightly floured surface. Wrap meat in dough to form rolls 3 inches long, seal and put in a large baking pan, seam side down. Do not crowd in pan. Let them rise until double in size. Bake at 400° for 15 minutes, then at 350° for 45 minutes. Brush tops with melted butter and serve. Serves 8.

HAMBURGER IN A SKILLET

Mix

¾ lb hamburger	2 tbsp minced onion
¼ cup dry bread crumbs	¾ tsp salt
1 egg, slightly beaten	¼ tsp dry mustard
¼ cup milk	⅛ tsp pepper

Form into 12 balls and sprinkle with flour. Brown on all sides in a skillet with 2 tbsp cooking oil. Place balls around edge of skillet, and in the middle pour 1 can condensed tomato soup mixed with ¾ cup condensed beef bouillon. Top with 1 package frozen mixed vegetables (thawed) and ½ tsp salt. Simmer for about 12 minutes. Serves 4.

VARIATION: Eliminate tomato soup and beef bouillon and add 1 can condensed cream of mushroom soup mixed with ¾ cup milk.

HAMBURGER SKILLET DINNER

Cut up 3 strips of bacon and fry until crisp. Add 1 lb hamburger and 2 chopped large onions and brown. Add ¼ cup soy sauce, ¼ tsp pepper, and ½ cup water. Add the following vegetables in layers: 2 sliced potatoes, 1 large sliced green pepper, 2 sliced tomatoes, 3 sliced stalks celery, and 2 cups chopped cabbage. Cover and cook over a high heat for 1 minute. Reduce heat and cook slowly for 15 minutes more. Serves 6.

HAMBURGER SMOKIES FOR FIFTY

Mix

13 lbs hamburger	¼ cup salt
3 cups chopped onion	1 tbsp pepper

Form into 50 patties and brown on both sides. Place patties in four pans and cover with thinly sliced onions.

Mix

2 qts catsup	2 tsp hot chili powder
½ cup white sugar	2 tsp liquid smoke
¼ cup brown sugar	2 tsp marjoram
2 cups vinegar	1 tsp oregano
4 tsp dry mustard	

Pour over patties and bake at 350° for 1½ hours. Baste occasionally. Serves 50.

HAMBURGER STROGANOFF

Sauté ½ cup chopped onions in ¼ cup butter until soft.

Add

1 lb hamburger	¼ tsp pepper
1 lb sliced mushrooms	½ tsp paprika
2 tbsp flour	¼ tsp monosodium
1 minced clove garlic	glutamate
1½ tsp salt	

Stir and sauté until hamburger loses its red color, then add 1 can condensed cream of chicken soup and simmer for 10 minutes. Stir in 1 cup sour cream. Serve on toast, topped with chopped parsley. Serves 6.

VARIATIONS: Eliminate mushrooms and chicken soup.

1. Add 1 can of condensed cream of mushroom soup. Serve over noodles and top with chopped chives.

2. Add 1 can of condensed cream of celery soup. Serve over mashed potatoes and top with chopped chives.

3. Add 1 can of condensed cream of mushroom soup. Serve over cooked rice and top with snipped fresh dill.

HAMBURGER-SPAGHETTI BAKE

In 2 tbsp cooking fat brown 1 lb hamburger, ¾ cup chopped onions, and ½ cup diced green pepper. Add

1 can condensed cream of mushroom soup	1 soup can of water
1 can condensed cream of tomato soup	1 mashed clove garlic

Stir in ½ cup grated sharp Cheddar cheese and ½ lb spaghetti, cooked according to directions on package. Place all in a 3-qt casserole and top with ½ cup grated sharp Cheddar cheese. Bake at 350° for about 30 minutes. Serves 6.

HAMBURGER-SPAGHETTI GOULASH

Fry 6 chopped strips of bacon.

Add

2 lbs hamburger	1 2-oz can mushrooms
¾ cup chopped onion	1 tsp salt
½ cup chopped green pepper	½ tsp pepper

Cook until meat loses its color, then add 3½ cups canned tomatoes, ½ tsp chili powder and ¼ tsp sage. Let simmer. Cook 1 lb spaghetti according to directions on package, add to sauce, and simmer for 30 minutes. Serve with grated Parmesan cheese. Serves 8.

HAMBURGER AND SPINACH

In 1 tbsp butter, brown 1 lb hamburger and 1 crushed clove garlic. Add 1 package frozen spinach and ½ tsp oregano. Cover and cook until spinach thaws. Add 4 eggs, slightly beaten, 2 tbsp grated Parmesan cheese, 1 tsp salt, and ¼ tsp pepper. Cook for 10 minutes more. Sprinkle 2 tbsp grated Parmesan cheese over top and serve. Serves 4.

HAMBURGER-STUFFED CABBAGE

Cook 10 large cabbage leaves in boiling salted water about 5 minutes until tender. In 2 tbsp cooking fat, brown 1 lb hamburger, ¼ cup minced green pepper, ½ cup chopped onion, 1 cup cooked rice, and 1½ tsp salt. Now mix in a kettle

1 cup water	1 tbsp brown sugar
1 tbsp wine vinegar	6 whole cloves
½ tsp dry mustard	2 bay leaves

Bring to a boil. Place heaping tbsp of meat mixture in each cabbage leaf, roll, tie with a string, and place in the boiling sauce. Simmer for 30 minutes. Serves 4.

HAMBURGER-STUFFED   CABBAGE
UNDER SAUERKRAUT

Remove the core from a large head of cabbage and place cabbage in enough boiling water to cover. Cut and remove leaves as they wilt. Trim thick center veins of each leaf. In a skillet with 3 tbsp cooking fat, sauté 1 cup minced onion. Add and brown 1 lb hamburger and ½ lb ground lean pork.

Add

¾ lb uncooked rice	2 tbsp salt
1 tbsp paprika	1 tsp black pepper

Place a heaping tbsp of mixture on each cabbage leaf and roll up. Place in a kettle and cover ⅔ full with water. Spread 1 No. 2 can sauerkraut on top of cabbage and pour 1 No. 2 can tomato juice over all. Cover and cook for 30 minutes. Pour ½ pint sour cream over all and heat for about 4 minutes. Serves 6 to 8.

HAMBURGER-STUFFED CHINESE CABBAGE

Mix

1¼ lbs hamburger	¼ cup chopped parsley
¼ lb ground lean pork	¼ cup chopped celery
1 cup canned tomatoes	1 tsp salt
¾ cup minced onion	¼ tsp pepper
¼ cup uncooked rice	

Cut stem end from large stalk Chinese cabbage, rinse leaves, and fill each leaf with meat mixture. Tie leaves together in original stalk form and place in a baking dish. Melt 3 tbsp butter, stir in 3 tbsp flour and 1 cup condensed beef bouillon. Stir and cook until thick. Add ½ tsp soy sauce, 1 cup tomato sauce, ¼ cup sliced dill pickle, and ½ tsp paprika. Cook for 3 minutes more. Add sauce to cabbage, cover, and bake at 350° for 1½ hrs. Serves 6.

HAMBURGER-STUFFED EGGPLANT

Cut an eggplant in two lengthwise and scoop out inside, leaving ¾ of an inch all around shell. Chop the scooped-out eggplant and cook in ¼ cup butter until clear. Add ½ cup chopped onion and 1 minced clove garlic. Cool and add 1¼ cups fine bread crumbs, ¾ lb hamburger, and 1 egg, slightly beaten. Heap the eggplant shells with the mixture, sprinkle with bread crumbs, and top with butter. Bake at 325° until meat mixture is done. Serve with tomato sauce mixed with horseradish. Serves 4.

HAMBURGER-STUFFED MUSHROOMS

Clean 1 lb fresh large mushrooms, remove and chop stems. In a large skillet with 1 tbsp cooking fat sauté ¼ cup minced onion and add ¼ lb hamburger, the mushroom stems, and ½ minced clove garlic. When lightly browned, add ½ tsp salt, ¼ tsp pepper, and 1 tbsp finely chopped parsley. Fill the mushroom caps, place in a greased baking dish, and bake at 375° for 25 minutes. To make sauce, melt 3 tbsp butter and add ¼ cup minced onion and ½ crushed clove garlic. Stir in 1 tbsp flour and add ½ cup dry white wine, 1 tbsp finely chopped dill pickle, 1 tbsp lemon juice, and ¼ tsp dry mustard. Just before serving, stir in ¾ cup sour cream. Pour over mushrooms. Serves 4.

HAMBURGER-STUFFED TOMATOES

Hollow out 6 unpeeled tomatoes and sprinkle with salt, pepper, sugar, and bread crumbs. Drop a little butter in bottom of each and arrange closely in a shallow baking dish. Brown ¾ lb hamburger in 1 tbsp cooking fat and mix with 1 tbsp minced onion, ¼ cup fine dry bread crumbs, ¾ tsp salt, and ⅛ tsp pepper. Moisten with the chopped pulp from tomatoes and fill shells with the mixture. Sprinkle with bread crumbs and dot with butter. Bake at 325° until tops are browned and tomato soft but not broken. Serves 6.

HOBO BURGERS

On a 12-inch square of aluminum foil, place 1 4-oz hamburger patty seasoned with salt and pepper, 1 thick slice onion, 1 thick slice tomato, ¼ of a green pepper, and 1 medium-sized potato, peeled, quartered, and rubbed with butter, salt and pepper. Seal foil and bake at 425° for about 45 minutes. Serves 1.

BARBECUED HAMBURGER PIES

Mix

2 lbs hamburger	¼ cup minced celery
1 lb ground lean pork	¼ cup minced parsley
1 lb liver sausage	1 tbsp salt
¼ cup chopped green pepper	1 tsp paprika
1 cup stale bread crumbs in	½ tsp pepper
1 cup red wine	½ tsp monosodium
1 crushed clove garlic	glutamate
¼ cup chopped onion	

Form into 12 loaves 2 inches thick and put in baking pan.

Barbecue Sauce:

1 cup catsup	2 tsp prepared mustard
½ cup wine vinegar	1 tsp chili powder
1 mashed clove garlic	1 tsp salt
¼ cup Worcestershire sauce	½ tsp liquid smoke

Beat well and let stand for 30 minutes. Pour over meat loaves and bake at 350° for 1 hour. Baste occasionally. Remove from pan, and when loaves are cool enough to handle, roll each loaf in a thin piecrust. Seal edges and prick top. Bake at 425° for 10 minutes, brush with butter, and bake 10 minutes more. Serve hot or cold. Serves 12.

HAMBURGER UPSIDE-DOWN PIE

In 2 tbsp cooking fat, brown 1 lb hamburger, ½ cup chopped onion, and ¼ cup diced green pepper until onion is transparent.

Add

1 8-oz can tomato sauce	1 tsp salt
1 can chopped ripe olives	1 tsp chili powder
¼ cup water	⅛ tsp black pepper

Pour into a 9-inch piepan. Cover with a biscuit dough prepared according to directions on package. Prick the top and bake at 425° for 20 minutes. Remove from oven and invert over serving dish. Serves 4 to 6.

HAMBURGER-WHEAT GERM RING

Mix

1 lb hamburger	4 tbsp chopped onion
1 egg, slightly beaten	1 tbsp chopped green pepper
½ lb ground lean pork	3 tbsp prepared horseradish
1 cup wheat germ	1 tsp prepared mustard
¾ cup milk	1 tsp salt

Place in greased 1½-qt ring mold. Place in pan of hot water and bake at 375° for 1¼ hours. Unmold and brown under broiler for 10 minutes. Fill center of ring with your favorite vegetables. Serves 6.

HAMBURGER AND WHEAT GERM PEPPERS

In ¼ cup bacon drippings, sauté

1 lb hamburger	¼ cup chopped celery
⅓ cup chopped onion	

Combine with

1½ cups drained cooked tomatoes	1 tsp salt
½ cup wheat germ	⅛ tsp pepper
1 cup bread crumbs	1 tsp chili powder

Slice 3 large green peppers in half lengthwise. Parboil for 5 minutes, drain, and fill with meat mixture. Bake in greased baking dish at 400° for 30 minutes. Serves 6.

BARBECUED MEAT BALLS AND BEANS

In a 2-qt casserole, mix

3 cups canned baked beans	2 tbsp brown sugar
1 pkg frozen lima beans, thawed	2 tsp dry mustard
2½ cups drained kidney beans	1 tsp salt
	⅛ tsp pepper

Bake at 400° for 45 minutes. In the meantime, parboil 8 or 10 small white onions.

Mix

1 lb hamburger	1 tsp salt
¼ cup minced onion	¼ tsp pepper
1 egg, slightly beaten	

Form into 12 balls and brown in a skillet with 1 tbsp cooking fat; remove from skillet. Wipe out skillet and add

⅔ cup catsup	1 tbsp butter
1 tbsp vinegar	¼ tsp dry mustard
2 tsp brown sugar	The meat balls

Simmer for 20 minutes, place meat balls and onions on top of beans, and top with the remaining sauce. Bake for 15 minutes more. Serves 6.

EARLY AMERICAN CHOP SUEY FOR ONE HUNDRED

Brown 15 lbs hamburger in a heavy kettle. Add 3 qts chopped onions and cook until soft:

Add

3 No. 10 cans tomatoes	6 tbsp salt
1 No. 10 can tomato purée	3 tsp pepper

Cook slowly for 35 minutes.

Boil 6 lbs macaroni in salted water according to directions on package. Drain, rinse in hot water, and drain again. Combine meat mixture and macaroni and divide into 5 greased baking pans. Sprinkle with grated American cheese and bake at 375° for about 20 minutes. Serves 100.

ELAINE'S CHILI

Sauté 1 minced clove garlic and 1 cup chopped onion in 2 tbsp cooking oil. Add 1 lb hamburger and cook until brown.

Add

1 No. 2½ can tomatoes	¼ tsp chili powder
1 No. 303 can kidney beans	1 tsp salt
¼ tsp cuminseed	¼ tsp pepper

Cover and simmer for 1½ hours. Serves 4.

SIMPLE CHILI AND BEANS

Sauté 1½ lbs hamburger, ½ cup chopped onions, and 1 tsp salt in large skillet until hamburger is browned.

Add

1 16-oz can kidney beans	1 tbsp chili powder
1½ qts tomato juice	¼ tsp pepper
1 tbsp beef extract	½ oz baking chocolate

Cover and simmer for 1½ hours. Stir occasionally. Serve with thin onion slices and lots of crackers. Serves 6.

MEAT BALLS WITH FRUIT FOR TWO

Mix

½ lb hamburger	⅙ tsp pepper
¼ cup bread crumbs	¼ tsp prepared mustard
3 tbsp milk	¼ tsp monosodium
½ tsp salt	glutamate

Form into balls and brown on all sides in a skillet. Serve on sautéed pineapple rings. Serves 2.

VARIATIONS: Serve on drained apricot halves, buttered and broiled.

Serve on drained peach halves, buttered and broiled.

RICE CON CARNE

In ¼ cup cooking fat, sauté until lightly browned

½ lb hamburger	¾ cup onion sliced thin
1⅓ cups minute-type rice	½ cup chopped green pepper

When browned, add

2 8-oz cans tomato sauce	1 tsp salt
1¾ cups hot water	⅛ tsp pepper
1 tsp prepared mustard	

Bring to a boil, cover and simmer for 15 minutes. Serves 4.

SPANISH HAMBURGER RICE

Brown ¾ cup regular raw rice in skillet with 2 tbsp cooking oil, then add

1 lb hamburger	½ cup chopped green pepper
¼ cup chopped onion	¼ cup chopped celery

Stir and cook until brown, then add

2½ cups cooked tomatoes	2 tsp salt
1 cup condensed beef bouillon	1 tsp soy sauce
½ tsp paprika	1 tsp sugar

Cover and simmer for 45 minutes. Sprinkle with snipped parsley. Serves 4.

TIMESAVER VARIATION: Use 1½ cups precooked rice in place of raw rice. Use 2 cans of tomato sauce in place of tomatoes. Reduce simmering time from 45 minutes to 10 minutes.

STUFFED CABBAGE WITH CHEESE SAUCE

Mix

¼ lb hamburger	¼ tsp salt
¼ cup cracker crumbs	⅛ tsp pepper

Remove heart from 1 head of cabbage and parboil leaves in salted water for about 10 minutes. Separate leaves carefully and stuff the meat mixture between leaves. Also stuff the center. Tie with a string, put in deep baking dish and add

⅓ cup chopped carrots	1 cup condensed beef bouillon
½ cup chopped onions	¼ cup butter

Bake at 350° for about an hour or until tender and meat is done. Serve topped with a cheese sauce. Serves 6.

STUFFED CABBAGE ROLLS

Pour boiling water over 12 large outside cabbage leaves, let stand until soft and pliable. Sauté ½ cup chopped onion in ½ lb butter until soft and clear. Add 1 lb hamburger, brown, and break up with a fork. Parboil the heart from the cabbage, chop, and add to the meat mixture.

Add

1 cup partially cooked rice	½ tsp paprika
⅓ cup seedless raisins	1 tsp salt
2 tbsp pine nuts	¼ tsp pepper

Let cool and mix in 1 slightly beaten egg. Fill cabbage leaves with meat mixture, secure so filling will not leak out. Cook 2 lbs sauerkraut and 1 lb pork spareribs in 1 quart water, salt and pepper, for 30 minutes. Place cabbage rolls on top of sauerkraut and cook covered for about 35 minutes more. Serves 6.

STUFFED GREEN PEPPERS

Cut tops from 4 large green peppers and remove seeds and fibrous portions. Cover with boiling salted water and simmer for 5 minutes. In the meantime, brown ½ lb hamburger and ¼ cup minced onions until meat loses its red color.

Add

1 tsp salt	2 cups cooked rice
¼ tsp pepper	1¼ cups canned tomatoes
¼ tsp powdered sage	1½ tsp bottled meat sauce

Stuff the pepper cases with the meat mixture, top with bread crumbs and melted butter. Bake at 375° for about 40 minutes or until tender and brown on top. Serves 4.

SPEEDY CHILI FOR TWO

Fry 2 slices chopped bacon with 2 tbsp chopped onion until brown. Brown ½ lb hamburger and add

½ cup cooked tomatoes	½ tsp chili powder
1 tbsp chili sauce	½ tsp salt
2 cups canned red kidney beans	⅛ tsp cayenne pepper

Cook for 15 minutes. Serves 2.

SWEDISH KALDOLMAR

Boil cabbage leaves for about 12 minutes or until tender, remove from water, and drain.

Mix

1 lb hamburger ground 3 times	1 tsp sugar
½ lb veal ground 3 times	1½ tsp salt
⅓ cup rice cooked in 1½ cups milk	¼ tsp pepper
1 egg, slightly beaten	½ tsp monosodium glutamate

Spoon meat mixture onto cabbage leaves, roll up, and tie with string. Brown the stuffed rolls in skillet with ¼ cup butter. Put rolls and drippings in Dutch oven, add ⅛ tsp allspice and simmer for 30 minutes, turning often. Serves 6.

TAGLIARINI

Sauté 1 cup chopped onions, ¾ cup chopped green pepper, and 2 crushed cloves garlic in 2 tbsp cooking fat until soft. Add 2 lbs hamburger and brown.

Add

2 cups drained canned tomatoes	1 tbsp salt
	½ tsp pepper
2 cups drained whole-kernel yellow corn	½ tsp allspice
	1 tsp monosodium
¼ cup tomato paste	glutamate
1 tsp oregano	

Cook slowly for 25 minutes. Stir in 1½ cups grated Cheddar cheese and 1 cup chopped pitted ripe olives. Serve over 1 package spaghetti, cooked according to directions on the package. Serves 8.

WHEAT BURGERS

Mix

1 lb hamburger	2 tbsp minced onion
¼ cup wheat germ	¾ tsp salt
⅓ cup milk	¼ tsp pepper

Form into 4 patties. Pan-fry or broil until done. Serves 4.

SOUTHWEST TAMALE PIE

Boil 2 cups hominy grits in 6 cups salted water for 30 minutes. In the meantime sauté

1 cup sliced onion	1 minced clove garlic
½ cup chopped green peppers	3 tbsp cooking fat

Cook until tender, then add 1 lb hamburger and ½ lb ground lean pork. Stir and cook until red color disappears, then add 2 cups condensed beef bouillon and 2 tbsp chili powder. Simmer for 45 minutes. On the bottom of a shallow baking dish spread a ½-inch layer of grits, 1-inch layer of meat mixture, layer of sliced ripe olives, and layer of grated Cheddar cheese. Repeat the layers and top with remaining grits. Cover and bake at 325° for 1 hour. Serves 8.

HAMBURGER AND EGG BREAKFAST

Form ¼ to ⅓ lb hamburger in a ring the shape of a doughnut and brown on both sides. Place 1 egg in the center hole of the hamburger ring. Cover and cook until egg is done the way you like it. Salt and pepper to taste. Serves 1.

HAMBURGER SUKIYAKI

Sauté 1 thinly sliced Bermuda onion in 1 tbsp salad oil in large heavy frying pan until it begins to soften. Add 1 lb hamburger and sauté 2 to 3 minutes, breaking up hamburger with a fork as it cooks.

Add

3 thinly sliced stalks celery	1 5-oz can drained bamboo
6 thinly sliced large fresh	shoots
mushrooms	1 tbsp sugar
¼ lb green beans, sliced	⅓ cup soy sauce
lengthwise	1 chicken bouillon cube
	½ cup water

Stir to mix, cover and simmer for 10 minutes. Clean and remove stems from ½ lb spinach and arrange on top of meat and vegetables. Cover and simmer 5 minutes longer, or until spinach wilts and vegetables are crisply tender. Serve with seasoned rice. Serves 6.

TAMALE PIE FOR FIFTY

Mix

2 lbs corn meal	3 tbsp salt
3 qts water	13 cups evaporated milk

Bring to a boil, stirring continuously, and cook until mixture thickens. Cover and set aside to cool.

Sauté 3 cups chopped onion and 6 lbs hamburger until brown. Add 1½ qts canned tomatoes, 5 tsp salt, and 2 tsp pepper. Cook for 20 minutes. Spread half of the corn meal mixture on bottom of greased 12 x 18 x 2-inch pan. Cover with meat mixture and top with balance of corn meal mixture. Bake at 375° for 45 minutes until top is lightly browned. Serves 50.

MEAT BALLS

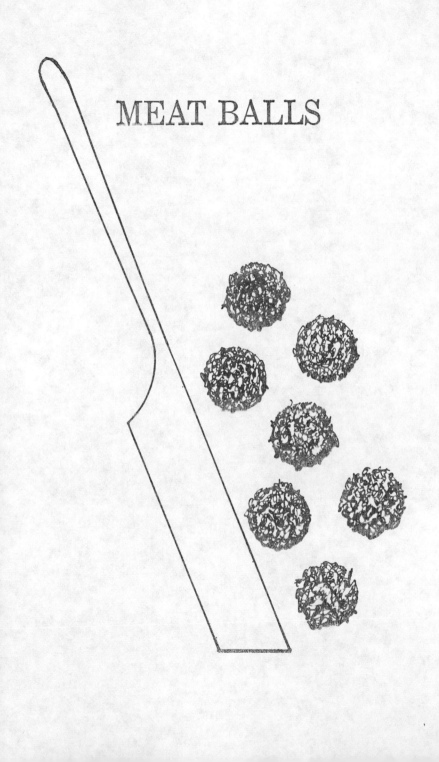

BAVARIAN MEAT BALLS

Mix

1 lb hamburger	2 tsp horseradish
¼ cup dry bread crumbs	1 tbsp catsup
1 egg, slightly beaten	1 tsp salt
¼ cup water	¼ tsp pepper
½ cup chopped onion	

Form into balls 1¼ inches in diameter and brown on all sides in 3 tbsp bacon drippings.

Mix

2 grated raw medium potatoes	¼ cup Rhine wine
2 apples, peeled and quartered	2 tsp brown sugar
2 cups sauerkraut	½ tsp salt
¼ cup chopped onion	⅛ tsp pepper
	⅛ tsp caraway seed

Place in casserole with meat balls on top. Cover and bake at 350° for 1 hour. Serves 4.

DANISH MEAT BALLS

Mix

1 lb hamburger ground 3 times	¾ cup flour
1¼ lbs lean pork ground 3 times	1¼ cups milk
	2 tsp salt
	¼ tsp pepper

Put all ingredients except meat in a mixer. Blend, adding meat gradually, until mixture is light and fluffy. Form into balls 1¼ inches in diameter and sauté in a skillet with 3 tbsp butter for about 15 minutes, turning constantly to brown on all sides. Serves 6.

DANISH MEAT BALLS WITH MASHED POTATOES

Mix

2 lbs hamburger	1 tsp ground nutmeg
1½ cups chopped onion	2 tsp salt
2 eggs, slightly beaten	½ tsp black pepper

Form into balls 1½ inches in diameter. Roll the meat balls in ⅔ cup flour seasoned with ¼ tsp salt and 1/16 tsp pepper. Brown on all sides in ¼ cup cooking fat. Add 1 cup condensed beef bouillon and 1 bay leaf. Cover and simmer for 30 minutes. Remove meat balls. Blend in 3 tbsp flour and brown. Stir in 1½ cups condensed beef bouillon. Cook, stirring constantly, until medium thick. Serve meat balls and gravy with mashed potatoes. Serves 6.

GERMAN MEAT BALLS

Sauté ¼ cup chopped onion and 1 crushed clove garlic in 1 tbsp butter and combine with

1 lb hamburger	2 egg yolks
⅓ cup bread crumbs in ½	1 tsp salt
cup milk	¼ tsp pepper
⅓ cup Rhine wine	¼ tsp nutmeg

Fold in 2 stiffly beaten egg whites.

Form into balls 1¼ inches in diameter, roll in flour, and brown on all sides in butter.

In a kettle, heat 2 generous cups of beer to boiling and add meat balls, 1 bay leaf, 1 tsp salt, ¼ tsp pepper, and ⅛ tsp marjoram. Cover and cook very slowly for 15 minutes. Add 4 cubed medium potatoes and 4 cubed carrots. Simmer until potatoes are done. Serve topped with chopped chives. Serves 4.

HUNGARIAN MEAT BALLS

Mix

1 lb hamburger	3 tbsp minced parsley
1 clove finely chopped garlic	¼ cup milk
½ cup dry bread crumbs	1 tsp salt
1 egg, slightly beaten	⅛ tsp pepper

Form into small balls and brown on all sides in ¼ cup cooking fat seasoned with 1 tsp Kitchen Bouquet. Remove meat balls and add

1 3-oz can chopped	2 cups sour cream
mushrooms	2 tbsp flour

Cook, stirring constantly, until thick. Add meat balls, cover, and cook slowly for 20 minutes. Serve over cooked noodles. Serves 4.

BROILED ITALIAN MEAT BALLS

Mix

1 lb hamburger	1 mashed clove garlic
1 egg, slightly beaten	1 tsp salt
1 cup cooked chopped	¼ tsp pepper
spinach	½ tsp monosodium
½ cup bread crumbs	glutamate
½ cup grated Parmesan	½ tsp oregano
cheese	

Form into balls 1½ inches in diameter. Roll in bread crumbs and broil in a greased shallow pan at 375° for 20 minutes, or until brown. Serves 4.

ITALIAN MEAT BALLS IN MUSHROOM SAUCE

Mix

¾ lb hamburger	2 crushed cloves garlic
½ lb ground lean pork	¼ tsp oregano
½ cup bread crumbs in ½	¼ tsp basil
cup milk	2 tbsp minced parsley
2 eggs, slightly beaten	1 tsp salt
4 tbsp grated Parmesan	¼ tsp pepper
cheese	

Form into 16 balls, roll in flour, and brown on all sides in 2 tbsp olive oil in skillet.

Mix

2 tbsp olive oil	½ cup celery chopped
3 cups sliced mushrooms	medium fine
½ cup chopped onion	½ tsp paprika
1 green pepper cut in 1-inch	½ tsp monosodium
squares	glutamate

Cover and cook over slow heat for 10 minutes.

Add

1 crushed clove garlic	1 crushed bay leaf
1 cup canned tomatoes	½ tsp salt
1 cup tomato juice	Pinch of pepper

Add meat balls to sauce and simmer for 40 minutes. Serves 4.

MEXICAN MEAT BALLS

Brown ½ cup bread crumbs in 1 tbsp bacon drippings and add

½ lb hamburger	2 tbsp minced parsley
½ lb ground lean pork	1 tsp cinnamon
2 chopped hard-boiled eggs	1 tsp salt
4 tbsp chopped onion	¼ tsp pepper

Form into balls 1 inch in diameter and set aside.

Mix 1 mashed clove garlic, ½ cup chopped onions, and ¼ cup chopped green pepper and sauté in 2 tbsp olive oil until tender. Add 1 8-oz. can tomato sauce, ½ 6-oz. can tomato paste, 2 cups water, 1 tsp chili powder, and ⅛ tsp salt and simmer for 30 minutes. Add meat balls and simmer for 1 hour. Serves 4.

MEXICAN MEAT BALLS IN CASSEROLE

Soak 2 slices bread in ¾ cup hot condensed beef bouillon, drain, and mix with

1 lb hamburger	dash of ground cloves
yolks from 2 hard-boiled eggs	dash of ground cinnamon
1 tsp salt	½ tsp monosodium
¼ tsp pepper	glutamate
dash of rosemary	

Form into balls 1 inch in diameter and cook slowly in 3 cups condensed beef bouillon seasoned with 2 tbsp chili powder for 30 minutes. Chop the whites from the 2 hard-boiled eggs. Mix with sauce and meat balls in a casserole. Top with 4 tbsp grated American cheese and bake at 350° for 20 minutes. Serves 4.

KOENIGSBERG MEAT BALLS

Mix

½ lb hamburger	2 eggs
½ lb ground veal	2 tbsp chopped onion
1 cup riced boiled potatoes	1 tbsp butter
1 tbsp anchovy paste	1 tbsp flour
¼ cup herring, chopped	1 tsp salt
very fine	¼ tsp pepper

Form into 12 round dumpling meat balls, roll in flour and set aside. To make gravy, place 1 cup chopped onion, 1 tbsp butter, 2 tbsp flour, and ¼ tsp salt in a cooking pan and sauté until onion is brown and flour is cooked. Add ⅔ tbsp vinegar and 3 cups water. Bring to a boil, place dumpling meat balls in gravy, and simmer for 10 minutes.

VARIATION: To the gravy, add 1 tbsp capers and 3 chopped anchovies or 2 tbsp chopped herring. One egg yolk may also be added. Serves 4.

NORWEGIAN MEAT BALLS AND GRAVY

Mix

2 lbs hamburger	1 tsp salt
2 eggs, slightly beaten	¼ tsp pepper
¾ cup flour	1 tsp nutmeg
1 cup milk	

Form balls 1¼ inches in diameter. In a skillet with ¼ cup cooking oil, brown balls well on all sides and put aside.

Sauté 1 cup chopped onions in same skillet as meat balls

were browned in. Combine onions with 2 cans condensed beef
bouillon and 2 cans water. Bring to a boil and add meat balls.
Simmer for 20 minutes. Remove meat balls from broth.

To make gravy, strain broth and thicken with 1 cup milk and
¼ cup flour. Season with 2 tbsp steak sauce. Pour gravy over
meat balls. Serves 8.

PERSIAN MEAT BALLS

Cook 2 cups coarse-ground cracked wheat in 5 cups heavily
salted water for about 45 to 50 minutes, or until it is the con-
sistency of pea soup. Sauté ¾ cup finely chopped onion in 3
tbsp butter and mix with

2 lbs hamburger (ground 4 times)	1 tsp paprika
1½ tsp salt	½ tsp tarragon
½ tsp dried mint	½ tsp monosodium glutamate

Form into meat balls about 2 inches in diameter and add to
the ground wheat mixture. Cook about 45 minutes and serve in
bowls. Serves 6 to 8.

RUMANIAN MEAT BALLS

Mix

2 lbs hamburger	⅓ cup condensed beef bouillon
2 eggs, slightly beaten	¼ tsp pepper
2 tbsp dill, chopped fine	1 tsp monosodium glutamate
2 tsp salt	
2 slices hard bread in ¼ cup milk	

Form into balls 1½ inches in diameter and dust lightly with
flour. Sauté until done in ⅓ cup butter. Serves 6.

RUMANIAN MEAT BALLS IN TOMATO SAUCE

Mix

2 lbs hamburger   1 crushed clove garlic
½ lb ground lean pork   ½ cup chopped parsley
2 eggs, slightly beaten   2 tsp salt
4 slices bread, soaked in   ½ tsp pepper
  water, squeezed dry

Form into balls 1 inch in diameter and brown in skillet, with ½ cup butter. Remove from skillet. In the remaining fat in skillet, sauté 2 cups chopped onions until soft.

Add

1 can condensed beef   1 8-oz can tomato sauce
  bouillon   6 bay leaves
2 cups Italian plum tomatoes   25 peppercorns

Simmer for 1 hour, add the meat balls and simmer for 45 minutes more. Serves 8.

RUSSIAN MEAT BALLS IN VODKA

Mix

2½ lbs hamburger   ½ tsp lemon rind
2 eggs, slightly beaten   ¼ tsp nutmeg
2 cups cracker crumbs   1 tsp salt
½ lb ground lean pork   ¼ tsp pepper
1 cup milk

Mix well and let stand for 1 hour, then form into small balls. Brown in a skillet in drippings along with 3 cups thinly sliced onions for about 15 minutes. Remove from pan. To the drippings, add 1 cup sour cream and thicken with 2 tbsp flour and 1 can condensed beef bouillon; cook until blended, then add onions and meat balls. Blend in ½ cup dry vermouth and 2 oz vodka. Serves 8 to 10—or 3 very hungry Russians.

SPANISH MEAT BALLS FOR FIFTY

Mix

13 lbs hamburger	2 oz salt
1 lb partially cooked rice	2 tbsp chili powder
12 eggs, slightly beaten	1 tsp cayenne pepper
1½ lbs mashed potatoes	1 tbsp monosodium
½ lb chopped green pepper	glutamate
4 oz minced onion	

Form into balls and place in large roasting pan. Cover with 3 qts tomato sauce and 2 qts tomato juice. Cover and cook at 350° for 2 hours. Serves 50.

SWEDISH MEAT BALLS IN BEER

Combine 1 slightly beaten egg and ¾ cup beer. Pour over 1½ cups bread crumbs. Sauté 3 tbsp finely chopped onion in 1 tbsp butter until soft, not brown. Mix with egg, beer, and bread crumbs.

Add

¾ lb hamburger, ground twice	1 tsp salt
	⅛ tsp pepper
¼ lb pork ground twice	⅛ tsp allspice
¼ lb veal ground twice	

Shape into 1-inch meat balls and roll in flour. Melt 3 tbsp butter in skillet and brown meat balls on all sides. Remove meat balls from pan and pour off all but two tbsp of the fat. Mix in 2 tbsp flour and cook till flour is brown. Gradually add 1 cup milk, stirring until gravy thickens and comes to a boil. Sprinkle with nutmeg and serve. Serves 8.

SWEDISH MEAT BALLS IN BURGUNDY

Sauté ½ cup grated onion in 1 tbsp cooking oil. Remove onion and mix with

1 lb hamburger	1 cup milk
1 cup bread crumbs	1 tsp salt
1 tsp cornstarch	Dash of mace
1 egg, slightly beaten	

Shape into about 40 tiny meat balls. Sauté until brown in drippings. Remove balls. Stir 3 tbsp flour into fat in pan. Add 1 cup water and 2 cups Burgundy wine. Place balls back in gravy and simmer about 20 minutes. Serves 6.

SWEDISH MEAT BALLS 3

Mix

1 lb hamburger	½ tsp chopped onion
½ lb ground veal	1 tsp chopped parsley
¼ lb ground fresh pork butt	1 tsp salt
½ cup toast crumbs	¼ tsp pepper
2 eggs, slightly beaten	½ tsp nutmeg
⅓ cup milk	

Shape into meat balls 1½ inches in diameter and roll in flour. Brown in 5 tbsp cooking oil in skillet. When brown, add 1 can condensed beef bouillon. Cover and cook 15 minutes more. Serves 8.

SWEDISH MEAT BALLS 4

Pour 1 cup milk over 2 cups bread crumbs and let stand for 5 minutes. Then mix with

1½ lbs hamburger	⅛ tsp allspice
½ lb ground veal	1/16 tsp ground cloves
2 eggs, slightly beaten	½ tsp monosodium
¼ cup finely chopped onion	glutamate
2 tsp salt	

Form into balls 1 inch in diameter and place in a skillet with 3 tbsp hot fat. Brown on all sides, then place in a casserole. Put 1½ tbsp flour and ½ tsp salt in the skillet. Add 1½ cups water, cook until thick, stirring constantly. Pour over meat balls, cover, and bake at 350° for 1 hour. Serves 6.

SWEDISH MEAT BALLS 5

Sauté ½ cup chopped onions in 2 tbsp butter in a large skillet. In mixing bowl, beat 1 egg slightly, add ½ cup milk and ½ cup bread crumbs. Let stand 10 minutes.

Add

1 lb hamburger	1¼ tsp salt
¼ lb ground pork shoulder	½ tsp allspice
2 tsp sugar	½ tsp nutmeg
Sautéed onions	

Form into small balls about ¾ inch in diameter. Heat 2 more tbsp butter in skillet and brown balls on all sides. Remove and place in casserole. In skillet, combine

3 tbsp flour	⅛ tsp pepper
1 tsp sugar	¾ cup water
1¼ tsp salt	¾ cup light cream

Stir until thickened, pour over meat balls. Serves 6.

SWEDISH MEAT BALLS 6

Mix

1 lb hamburger	½ cup finely chopped onions
1 lb ground veal	1½ tsp salt
2 eggs, slightly beaten	¼ tsp pepper
½ cup chopped ripe olives	½ tsp nutmeg

Form into small balls and brown in 2 tbsp butter. Remove from pan and keep hot. In same skillet, combine 2 cups sour cream and 1 tsp dill seed. Reheat, stirring constantly. Pour over meat balls and serve. Serves 8.

SWEDISH MEAT BALLS 7

Mix

1 lb hamburger	1½ tsp brown sugar
½ lb ground lean pork	½ tsp white pepper
1 egg, slightly beaten	1½ tsp salt
1 cup milk	1 tsp nutmeg
¾ cup dry bread crumbs	½ tsp allspice
¼ cup minced onions	

Form into small balls 1 inch in diameter, roll in flour, brown on all sides in ¼ cup butter. Add 1 cup cream and ¼ cup beer. Cover, bring to a boil, simmer for 15 minutes. Serves 6.

SWEDISH MEAT BALLS FOR TWO

Mix

½ lb hamburger	¼ cup water
1 egg, slightly beaten	⅔ tsp salt
3 tbsp bread crumbs	⅛ tsp pepper

Sauté 3 tbsp chopped onion in 2 tbsp hot fat. Strain. Mix onion with meat mixture, form into small balls, and brown on all sides in hot fat. Transfer the balls to another pan. Cover with gravy made with 1 tbsp flour, browned in remaining fat, and 1 cup condensed beef bouillon, stirring until gravy boils. Season with salt, pepper, Kitchen Bouquet, and ground nutmeg. Simmer for 30 minutes. Serves 2.

> VARIATION: Shape meat-ball mixture into 4 rolls and brown in hot fat. Form 4 squares of prepared biscuit dough. Place a meat roll on each piece of dough and form dough firmly around meat. Brush with milk and bake at 400° for 15 minutes. Top with mushroom soup.

SWEDISH MEAT BALLS FOR FIFTY

Mix

13 lbs hamburger	3 oz salt
2½ lbs bread in 1½ qts milk	1 oz pepper
12 eggs, slightly beaten	1 oz nutmeg
1½ lbs grated raw potatoes	1 oz monosodium
1 lb chopped onions	glutamate

Form into balls and brown in oven at 400° for 15 minutes. Bake at 350° for 1 hour. Make a cream gravy from meat drippings and pour over meat balls. Serves 50.

ALMOND MEAT BALLS

Sauté 4 tbsp chopped onion in 1 tbsp olive oil and add ½ cup tomato purée, 1 cup water, and ½ tsp salt.

Sauté 1 cup blanched almonds, 1 small mashed clove garlic and 1 slice cubed bread in 3 tbsp olive oil. Cool, grind through meat grinder with medium blade, add to tomato mixture and simmer for 15 minutes.

Mix

1 lb hamburger	1 egg, slightly beaten
¼ lb lean ground pork	1 tsp salt
2 slices bread cubes in ¼ cup hot milk	⅛ tsp pepper
	3 tsp chili powder

Cut 2 hard-boiled eggs lengthwise in quarters, then cut the quarters in half. Divide the meat to make 16 balls, and form the meat around each piece of egg. Brown on all sides and add to sauce. Simmer for 20 minutes. Top with ½ cup sliced blanched toasted almonds. Serves 4.

APPLESAUCE MEAT BALLS

Mix

1 lb hamburger	½ cup chopped onion
1 egg, slightly beaten	¾ tsp salt
¼ cup applesauce	⅛ tsp pepper
½ cup crushed corn flakes	⅛ tsp garlic salt

Form into small balls and place in open roasting pan. Top with 1 8-oz can tomato sauce and bake at 350° for 1 hour. Stir frequently. Serves 4.

BURGUNDY MEAT BALLS

Mix

¾ lb hamburger	¾ tsp cornstarch
¾ cup bread crumbs	¾ tsp salt
½ cup chopped onion	¼ tsp pepper
1 egg, slightly beaten	⅛ tsp nutmeg
¾ cup light cream	⅛ tsp allspice

Form into 30 balls and brown on all sides in skillet in ¼ cup cooking oil. Remove balls. Stir 3 tbsp flour into fat in skillet, then stir in

2 beef bouillon cubes in 2	½ tsp salt
cups water	⅛ tsp pepper
1 cup Burgundy wine	

Stir until smooth and add the meat balls. Cover and simmer for 30 minutes. Serves 6.

BURGUNDY MEAT BALL STEW

Mix

2 lbs hamburger	1 crushed clove garlic
2 eggs, slightly beaten	2 tbsp minced parsley
1 cup bread crumbs in ½	2 tsp salt
cup Burgundy	½ tsp pepper
¼ cup minced onion	

Form into 32 balls, roll in flour and brown on all sides in skillet with ⅓ cup butter. Add 3 cups boiling water, 5 cloves, and 1 cup Burgundy. Cover and simmer for 20 minutes.

Add

4 cups cubed potatoes	16 small white onions
2 cups cubed carrots	2 cups sliced celery

Cover and simmer for 30 minutes until vegetables are done. Remove cloves. Serves 8.

BUTTERMILK MEAT BALLS

Mix

1½ lbs hamburger	1 cup cooked rice
½ cup chopped onion	1 tsp salt
4 tbsp chopped green pepper	1 egg, slightly beaten
⅓ cup sliced celery	½ tsp pepper

Shape into 12 meat balls. Place into greased 2-qt casserole.

Mix until smooth, using beater

1 can condensed cream of   Liquor from 2-oz can of
  mushroom soup   mushrooms
1 soup can of buttermilk

Pour over meat balls along with mushrooms from 2-oz can and bake at 350° for 1 hour. Serves 6.

CHIFFON MEAT BALLS

Mix in an Osterizer or other blender

1 egg   ¼ tsp paprika
1 small potato, cut up   ¼ tsp marjoram
1 quartered onion   ¼ tsp pepper
1 carrot, cut up   ½ tsp monosodium
½ clove garlic   glutamate
1 tsp salt

Blend for about 4 minutes and mix with 1 lb hamburger and ⅓ cup dry bread crumbs. Form into balls 1¼ inches in diameter and set aside. Sauté 2 cups sliced onions in 3 tbsp butter until tender. Place meat balls on top of onions, cover, and simmer for 30 minutes. Serves 4.

COCKTAIL MEAT BALLS

Mix

½ lb hamburger   ⅛ tsp nutmeg
4 tbsp bread crumbs   ⅛ tsp Tabasco
2 tbsp mayonnaise   ½ tsp salt
2 tsp minced onion   ¼ tsp pepper
¼ tsp horseradish

Form into 24 tiny balls. Brown in 2 tbsp bacon drippings. Drain and roll each ball in grated American cheese. Insert picks in meat balls. Serve hot. Makes 24 meat balls.

VARIATION: Serve without cheese, in pan gravy thickened with 2 tbsp flour and ½ cup milk. Serve with picks.

COUNTRY MEAT BALLS AND VEGETABLES

Mix 1½ cups bread cubes in ⅓ cup milk and squeeze dry. Combine with

1 lb hamburger	1 tsp salt
½ cup chopped onion	¼ tsp pepper
1 egg, slightly beaten	

Form into 24 small balls and brown in 2 tbsp butter. Remove from skillet. Heat ⅓ cup cooking fat in Dutch oven.

Add

2 crushed cloves garlic and 1 cup sliced onions. Cook until onions are soft.

Add

4 sliced zucchini and 1 diced eggplant. Cover and simmer 30 minutes. Stir frequently.

Add

2 green peppers cut in strips, 2 tsp salt, and ¼ tsp pepper. Cook for 15 minutes.

Add meat balls and 5 quartered ripe tomatoes. Cook for 10 minutes. Serves 4.

COCKTAIL MEAT BALLS IN BARBECUE DIP

Sauté ¼ cup minced onion in 2 tbsp butter until soft. Do not brown. Stir in

½ cup chili sauce	1 tsp dry mustard
1 8-oz can tomato sauce	1 tsp chili powder
1 4½-oz can chopped ripe olives	1 tsp Worcestershire sauce
	¼ tsp Tabasco
2 tsp horseradish	

Blend dip well and place in serving dish. To make meat balls, mix

1 lb hamburger	1 cup cracker crumbs
1 egg, slightly beaten	1¼ tsp salt
1 cup milk	¼ tsp pepper
2 tbsp grated onion	

Form into tiny balls and brown in 2 tbsp cooking oil. Insert wooden pick in each ball and serve with barbecue sauce dip. Serves 4.

CREAMED MEAT BALLS ON TOAST

Mix

1 lb hamburger	½ tsp salt
½ cup bread crumbs in ½ cup milk	⅛ tsp pepper
	½ tsp monosodium
¼ tsp nutmeg	glutamate

Form into ball ¾ inch in diameter and brown on all sides in skillet with 2 tbsp butter. Put aside. In another pan, mix

¼ cup melted butter	2 tbsp chopped parsley
1 cup sliced mushrooms	¼ cup finely chopped
2 tbsp minced onion	pimiento
1 crushed clove garlic	

Simmer for about 5 minutes. Stir in ¼ cup flour. Stirring constantly, add 1 cup condensed beef bouillon, 1 cup milk, ¾ tsp salt, ¼ tsp pepper. Add meat balls, stir and simmer for about 6 minutes. Add 2 tbsp port wine and serve on toast. Serves 6.

CREOLE MEAT BALLS AND NOODLES

Mix

½ lb hamburger	½ tsp salt
1 egg, slightly beaten	⅛ tsp pepper
⅓ cup dry bread crumbs	

Form into balls and brown in a large skillet with 2 tbsp cooking fat.

Add

¼ cup chopped onions	1 tbsp sugar
¼ cup chopped celery	1 tsp salt
2½ cups canned tomatoes	¼ tsp black pepper
1 tbsp Worcestershire sauce	

Cover and simmer for 30 minutes. In the meantime, cook 6 oz broad noodles according to directions on package. Cream 3 tbsp flour in 2 tbsp butter and stir into meat ball mixture. Cook until thick, stirring constantly. Serve over noodles. Serves 4.

DIETETIC MEAT BALLS

Mix

1 lb lean hamburger	¼ cup minced green pepper
¼ cup grated onion	1 tsp Angostura bitters
1 slightly beaten egg	1 tsp salt
¼ cup wheat germ	¼ tsp pepper

Form into small balls 1 inch in diameter. Sprinkle ¼ tsp salt in a skillet and brown meat balls on all sides. Salt will keep meat balls from sticking to skillet. When browned, remove any fat from skillet and add 1 10½-oz can condensed beef bouillon. Cover and simmer for 20 minutes. Serves 4.

DUTCH OVEN MEAT BALLS

Mix

1 lb hamburger	1 tsp salt
1 egg, slightly beaten	⅛ tsp pepper
½ cup bread crumbs	⅛ tsp allspice
¼ cup tomato sauce	1 tsp onion juice

Shape into 12 meat balls. Brown on all sides with 2 tbsp cooking oil in a Dutch oven.

Add

3 cups water	1 1½-oz pkg onion soup mix
¾ cup tomato sauce	1½ cups sliced carrots
1 10-oz pkg frozen peas	1 cup cubed green pepper
3 medium potatoes, cubed	

Bring to a boil and cook over a low heat for 30 minutes until vegetables are done. Serves 4.

HAMBURGER POTATO BALLS

Cook 3 medium potatoes in jackets, peel, and put through a ricer. While warm, mix with

1½ lbs hamburger	3 tbsp chopped parsley
¼ cup chopped onion	1½ tsp salt
2 eggs, slightly beaten	¼ tsp pepper
1 small chopped clove garlic	½ tsp paprika

Form into balls 1 inch in diameter and roll in flour. Cook in a skillet with ¼ cup cooking oil until done, about 12 minutes. Serves 6.

HAMBURGER TOMATO BALLS

Mix

1½ lbs hamburger	1½ tsp salt
1 egg, slightly beaten	¼ tsp pepper
2 tbsp minced onion	

Form into balls 1 inch in diameter and brown on all sides in hot fat. Set aside. Melt 2 tbsp butter, stir in 3 tbsp flour, and add 2 cups strained tomatoes, stirring constantly until thickened.

Add

⅛ tsp pepper	½ tsp salt
½ tsp prepared mustard	¼ tsp Worcestershire sauce
½ cup grated cheese	1 tbsp sugar

Stir until cheese melts and pour over meat balls. Cover and simmer for 20 minutes. Serves 6.

LEMON MEAT BALLS IN CREAM SAUCE

Mix

1½ lbs hamburger	1 tsp celery salt
1 cup bread crumbs	1 tsp Worcestershire sauce
2 tsp grated lemon rind	1 tsp salt
2 eggs, slightly beaten	¼ tsp pepper
¾ cup milk	½ tsp monosodium
2 tbsp chopped onion	glutamate
1 crushed clove garlic	

Form into 18 balls and brown on all sides in 3 tbsp butter. Remove from skillet and set aside. Simmer 1 cup chopped green pepper in skillet for 10 minutes. Stir in 2 tbsp flour and brown for about 3 minutes. Slowly add 1½ 8-oz cans tomato sauce, ½ can water, and ¼ tsp salt, stirring constantly. Add 1 cup sour cream. Pour sauce over meat balls and bake at 300° for 30 minutes. Serves 6.

MAINE MEAT BALL STEW

Mix

¾ lb hamburger	¼ cup tomato sauce
½ lb ground veal	½ tsp onion salt
1 egg, slightly beaten	¼ tsp pepper

Form into balls 1¼ inches in diameter and broil on all sides about 3 inches from heat source for about 10 minutes. Place in a kettle.

Add

1 cup white wine	1 cup canned tomatoes
1 vegetable bouillon cube in	½ cup chopped onions
¼ cup water	⅛ tsp sugar

Cover and simmer for 10 minutes. Add 1 package frozen succotash and simmer for about 25 minutes.

Add ½ cup croutons, 2 tbsp butter, 1 tsp salt, ⅛ tsp cayenne pepper, and serve. Serves 6.

MALIBU MEAT BALLS

Mix

1 lb hamburger	¼ cup chopped parsley
1 egg, slightly beaten	1 tsp salt
¼ cup bread crumbs	¼ tsp pepper
¼ cup milk	½ tsp powdered sage
½ cup chopped onion	

Form into balls and roll in corn meal.

To make sauce, sauté 1 cup chopped onion, ¾ cup chopped green pepper, and 1 chopped clove garlic in 2 tbsp bacon drippings for 5 minutes.

Add

2 tbsp flour	⅛ tsp thyme
½ cup dry red wine	⅛ tsp marjoram
1 No. 303 can tomatoes	1 crushed bay leaf
1 cup condensed beef bouillon	⅛ tsp salt
1 tbsp sugar	⅛ tsp pepper

Simmer for 1 hour. Add meat balls and simmer for another 45 minutes. Serve with spaghetti. Serves 6.

PANHANDLE MEAT BALLS

Mix

1 lb hamburger	¼ cup chopped parsley
2 oz crushed barbecued corn chips	½ tsp salt
	⅛ tsp pepper
½ cup finely chopped onion	¼ tsp marjoram
1 egg, slightly beaten	

Form into small balls and roll in 2 oz crushed barbecued corn chips. Fry meat balls 5 to 10 minutes until done. Serve with a mixture of catsup and horseradish. Serves 4.

PIQUANT MEAT BALLS

Put ¼ lb sharp cheese, ½ green pepper, and 12 stuffed olives through coarse food chopper and mix with

1 lb hamburger	1 tsp salt
1 egg, slightly beaten	⅛ tsp pepper
½ cup milk	½ tsp monosodium glutamate
4 tbsp lemon juice	
1 cup bread crumbs	

Form into 12 balls. Wrap each ball in ½ slice bacon, fasten with pick, bake in shallow dish at 400° for 30 minutes. Serves 4.

PAPRIKA MEAT BALLS

Sauté 1 clove garlic in 2 tbsp cooking fat and remove garlic.
Mix

2 lbs hamburger	1 tsp salt
1 egg, slightly beaten	¼ tsp paprika
2 tbsp Worcestershire sauce	

Form into small balls and brown in the fat. Add 1 cup water
and 2 tbsp Worcestershire sauce and cook slowly for 2 hours. Add
1 cup sour cream and 1 tsp paprika and cook for 15 minutes
more. Remove meat balls and thicken the gravy with 2 tbsp flour
in ½ cup of cold water. Stir and boil for 5 minutes. Pour gravy
over meat balls. Serves 6.

PINEAPPLE MEAT BALLS ON A SKEWER

Mix

¾ lb hamburger	1 cup bread crumbs
¾ lb ground pork	¼ cup milk
1 egg, slightly beaten	

Form into 18 balls. On 6 skewers place a meat ball, 2 pineapple
chunks, meat ball, 2 pineapple chunks and a meat ball. Place
skewers on bottom of shallow baking pan.

Mix

½ cup brown sugar	¼ cup water
¼ cup vinegar	½ tsp dry mustard

Stir until sugar dissolves and pour over meat balls, along
with excess pineapple chunks. Bake at 350° for 1 hour. Baste
often. Serves 6.

POTTED MEAT BALLS AND VEGETABLES

Mix

1½ lbs hamburger	1½ tsp salt
1 cup chopped onion	¼ tsp pepper
¼ cup uncooked rice	
1½ tbsp Worcestershire sauce	

Form into 12 balls and brown with 4 tbsp cooking fat in a Dutch oven. Remove balls and set aside. Pour fat from kettle.

Add

2 cans condensed tomato soup	1 tsp salt
	¼ tsp thyme
1 soup can of water	1 bay leaf
1 crushed clove garlic	

Bring to a boil and add

4 carrots cut into 1-inch pieces	18 small white onions
4 potatoes cut into 1-inch cubes	

Cover and simmer for 15 minutes, then place meat balls on top of vegetables. Cover and simmer 40 minutes. Serves 6.

RAISIN SAUCE MEAT BALLS

Mix

1½ lb hamburger	½ cup chopped onions
2 eggs, slightly beaten	1½ tsp salt
1 cup dry bread crumbs	¼ tsp pepper
¾ cup cream	¼ tsp allspice

Form into 24 balls and brown in a skillet with ¼ cup cooking oil. For sauce, mix

¼ cup bacon drippings	¾ cup chopped celery
½ cup chopped onions	1 crushed clove garlic

Simmer in a saucepan for 6 minutes, then add

1½ cups water	¾ tsp salt
1 cup seedless raisins	¼ tsp pepper
¼ cup tomato sauce	

Simmer for 30 minutes. Remove from fire and add ¼ cup dry red wine. Serve meat balls and sauce over noodles. Serves 6.

SAVORY MEAT BALLS

Mix

1 lb hamburger	1 tsp dry mustard
1 egg, slightly beaten	1 tsp salt
¼ cup chopped onion	¼ tsp pepper
½ cup milk	¼ tsp poultry seasoning
¼ cup corn meal	

Form into 16 small balls and roll in flour. Brown on all sides in 2 tbsp cooking fat. Place in casserole, sprinkle lightly with 2 tbsp flour, add 1½ cups tomato juice and bake at 350° for 45 minutes. Serves 4 to 6.

SOUTHERN MEAT BALLS AND NOODLES FOR FIFTY

Mix

7 lbs hamburger	2 tbsp salt
7 eggs, slightly beaten	1 tsp pepper
1½ cups bread crumbs	

Form into 100 balls. Brown balls on all sides in ¾ cup cooking fat or drippings. Add 4 cups chopped onion and 3 cups chopped celery and cook until light brown. Stir in

5 qts cooked tomatoes	2 tbsp salt
1 cup sugar	½ tsp pepper
2 tbsp Worcestershire sauce	1 tsp Louisiana hot sauce

Cover and simmer for 30 minutes. Cook 4 lbs noodles according to directions on package. Cream together 1 cup butter with 2 cups sifted flour and stir into meat ball mixture. Cook until thickened. Serve meat ball mixture over noodles. Serves 50.

STUFFED MEAT BALLS

Mix

½ lb hamburger	1 egg, slightly beaten
½ lb ground pork	½ cup bread crumbs
½ lb ground veal	1 tsp salt
½ cup chopped onion	½ tsp pepper

Form into 20 thin patties. Put a stuffed olive inside a pitted prune. Put stuffed prune between 2 meat patties to form meat balls. Brown on all sides in 2 tbsp hot fat in skillet. Add ½ cup milk to 1 can condensed cream of mushroom soup and pour over meat balls. Cook over low heat for 20 minutes. Serves 3 or 4.

SPAGHETTI AND MEAT BALLS FOR FIFTY

Mix

8 lbs hamburger	¾ cup minced parsley
8 eggs, slightly beaten	3 tbsp salt
4 cups bread crumbs	1½ tsp black pepper
3½ cups milk	

Form into balls 1¼ inches in diameter. Sauté 2 qts chopped onion, 1 qt chopped green pepper, and 16 mashed garlic cloves in 2½ cups olive oil. Add meat balls and brown on all sides.

Add

5 qts condensed tomato soup	1 tbsp salt
5 qts water	1 tbsp basil
1 cup lemon juice	1 tbsp sage
3 bay leaves	2 tsp thyme
½ cup sugar	2 tsp pepper

Simmer for 2 hours. Cook 8 lbs spaghetti in salted water according to directions on package. Combine 10 oz of sauce with each lb of cooked spaghetti. Sprinkle with Parmesan cheese. Serves 50.

TOMATO MEAT BALLS

Mix

1 lb hamburger	½ cup uncooked rolled oats
½ cup chopped onion	1 tsp salt
⅔ cup canned tomato juice	¼ tsp pepper

Form into 12 balls and brown well on all sides in skillet with 3 tbsp cooking fat. Add an 8-oz can tomato sauce and simmer for 30 minutes. Serve topped with chopped chives. Serves 6.

MEAT BALLS AND BAKED VEGETABLES

Mix

1 lb hamburger	1 egg, slightly beaten
1 cup bread crumbs	1 tsp salt
¼ cup chopped onion	¼ tsp pepper

Form into 12 meat balls, roll in flour, and brown all sides in 3 tbsp cooking fat. Add 3 tbsp flour to skillet meat balls were browned in. Add 2 cups canned tomatoes, 2 cups cubed raw potatoes, 1 cup sliced onions, ½ cup chopped celery, and 1 tsp salt. Place 6 meat balls in bottom of baking dish. Cover with half the vegetable mixture, then the other 6 meat balls, and top with other half of the vegetable mixture. Cover and bake at 350° for 1 hour. Garnish with parsley. Serves 6.

MEAT BALLS AND BARBECUED BEANS

Fry 6 strips bacon cut in small pieces in skillet until crisp and remove from skillet.

Mix

1½ lbs hamburger	1½ tsp salt
½ lb ground pork	½ tsp pepper

Form into balls and brown on all sides in the bacon fat. Then mix

¾ cup chili sauce	2 tbsp Worcestershire sauce
4 tbsp brown sugar	3 tbsp vinegar

Pour over the meat balls, add 1½ cups sliced onions. Stir occasionally and cook for 6 minutes. Put 2 cans barbecued beans or brown beans in a baking dish and mix in the crisp bacon pieces. Place meat balls and sauce on top and bake at 350° for 1 hour. Serves 8.

MEAT BALL BOBS

Mix

1 lb hamburger	¼ tsp pepper
1 tsp salt	

Form into 12 balls. On 4 skewers arrange meat ball, green pepper, half an onion, meat ball, green pepper, half an onion, meat ball. Brush with oil and broil until meat is cooked to taste. Serves 4.

MEAT BALLS CREOLE

Mix

2 lbs hamburger	2 tbsp salt
¼ cup chopped onion	½ tsp thyme
2 eggs, slightly beaten	⅓ tsp cayenne pepper
1 cup tomato juice	½ tsp monosodium
1 cup dry bread crumbs	glutamate
1 tbsp chili powder	

Form into balls 1¼ inches in diameter. Roll in flour and set aside. In ⅓ cup cooking fat, sauté 1 cup sliced onion, ¾ cup chopped green pepper, ½ cup chopped celery, and 3 cups sliced mushrooms and remove to large kettle. Brown meat balls in same pan, then add to kettle along with

5 cups canned tomatoes	⅓ tsp cayenne pepper
1 crushed bay leaf	¼ cup sweet wine
1 tsp salt	

Cover and simmer for 30 minutes. Thicken with 2 tbsp flour in ¼ cup water. Serves 8.

MEAT BALL GUMBO

Mix

2 lbs hamburger	2 tsp salt
¼ cup chopped onion	½ tsp thyme
1 cup tomato juice	¼ tsp cayenne pepper
2 eggs, slightly beaten	½ tsp monosodium
½ cup dry bread crumbs	glutamate
1 tbsp chili powder	

Form into balls 1¼ inches in diameter. Roll in flour and set aside. Sauté 1 cup sliced onions and 1 cup chopped green pepper in ¼ cup cooking fat and remove from skillet. Place meat balls in skillet and brown on all sides. Add onion and pepper, 5 cups tomatoes, 1 crushed bay leaf, 1 tsp salt, ½ tsp pepper, ¼ tsp basil. Cover and simmer for 10 minutes. Add 2 cups okra sliced in ½-inch pieces. Cover and simmer 20 minutes. Serves 8.

MEAT BALLS AND MUSHROOMS

Sauté 3 cups sliced mushrooms for 10 minutes in a skillet with 3 tbsp butter and 1 tsp paprika. Remove to another pan.

Mix

1 lb hamburger	½ tsp onion salt
1 tbsp thick meat sauce, such as A.1. or Heinz 57 Sauce	½ tsp celery salt

Form into 36 small balls and brown on all sides in same skillet. Remove and place with mushrooms. Pour off all but 3 tbsp drippings in a skillet and stir in 1 tbsp flour until blended. Stir in ½ can condensed beef bouillon; cook, stirring constantly, until smooth and thick. Add sauce to meat balls and mushrooms and simmer for 10 minutes. Serve over cooked rice. Serves 4.

MEAT BALLS AND SAUERKRAUT

Mix

1 lb hamburger	½ cup dry bread crumbs
1 lb ground lean pork	1½ tsp salt
1 egg, slightly beaten	½ tsp pepper

Form into balls and brown on all sides. Add 1 No. 303 can sauerkraut. Cover and cook 30 minutes. Add juice from 1 No. 303 can tomatoes. Cook 15 minutes. Add the tomatoes and 3 tsp sugar and cook 15 minutes more. Serves 6 to 8.

MEAT BALL CURRY

Mix

1 lb hamburger	½ tsp salt
½ cup canned tomatoes	½ tsp curry powder
¼ cup dry bread crumbs	

Form into 20 balls and brown on all sides in 2 tbsp cooking oil. Remove and place in kettle. In the skillet, add

1 cup condensed beef bouillon	⅓ cup seedless raisins
2 medium apples, cubed	1 tsp curry powder
⅔ cup chopped celery	¼ tsp ginger
3 tbsp chopped onion	½ tsp monosodium glutamate

Cook for about 2 minutes and pour over meat balls in kettle. Simmer for 15 minutes more. Slowly add 1 tbsp flour in ¼ cup water, stirring constantly, and simmer for 5 minutes more. Serve over boiled rice. Serves 4.

MEAT BALL MAC

Mix

1 lb hamburger	1 tsp salt
1 egg, slightly beaten	¼ tsp thyme
½ cup chopped onion	¼ tsp pepper
½ cup bread crumbs	

Form into 30 small balls and brown in 3 tbsp cooking fat in large frying pan. Add

3 cups water	¼ cup chopped onion
1 can condensed cream of mushroom soup	1½ tsp salt
1 8-oz can tomato sauce	⅛ tsp pepper
	1 bay leaf

Bring to a boil and add 8 oz thin spaghetti in ½-inch lengths. Cover and simmer for 30 minutes. Stir once in a while to keep spaghetti from sticking to pan. Serves 6.

MEAT BALL PIE FOR FIFTY

Mix

6 lbs hamburger	1 cup chili sauce
6 eggs, slightly beaten	¾ cup milk
2 tbsp salt	

Form into balls 1½ inches in diameter. Brown in ½ cup cooking oil. Remove balls and drain. To drippings in pan, add 1½ cups flour and 2 tbsp salt, mixing thoroughly. Add 2 qts vegetable juice. Stir until thick. Divide meat balls in 2 pans and add 1½ qts mixed vegetables to each pan. Top each pan with biscuit mix and bake at 450° for 25 minutes. Serves 50.

MEAT BALLS IN ONION GRAVY

Cook 3 cups sliced onions sprinkled with 1 tsp paprika in a skillet with ¼ cup butter. Cook, covered, until light brown. Remove to another cooking pan.

Mix

1½ lb hamburger	¼ tsp pepper
2 eggs, slightly beaten	¼ tsp celery salt
⅓ cup bread crumbs	¼ tsp garlic salt
2 tbsp catsup	½ tsp monosodium
½ cup water	glutamate
1 tsp salt	

Form into balls 1 inch in diameter and dust with flour. Add 2 tbsp butter to same skillet onions were cooked in and brown meat balls on all sides. Remove balls to same pan with onions. Brown 2 tbsp flour in drippings and gradually add 3 cups mixed vegetable juice. Cook until thick and smooth, pour over meat balls and onions, cover and simmer for 30 minutes. Garnish with chopped parsley. Serves 6.

MEAT BALLS IN PINEAPPLE SAUCE

Mix

2 lbs hamburger	2 tsp salt
1 slice bread crumbled in	½ tsp garlic salt
½ cup milk	½ tsp pepper
1 egg, slightly beaten	

Form into small balls and brown in 2 tbsp cooking oil, shaking pan often to keep balls round. Remove meat balls and set aside. To make pineapple sauce, mix

1 can condensed beef bouillon	½ cup sugar
	2 tbsp soy sauce
1 No. 2 can pineapple chunks and syrup	½ tsp salt
	1 tsp monosodium
½ cup chopped green pepper	glutamate
¼ cup wine vinegar	

Bring to a boil. Thin 2 tbsp cornstarch in water and stir into sauce. Simmer for about 15 minutes until sauce is clear and thick. Add meat balls and simmer for 15 minutes more. Serves 8.

MEAT BALLS AND POTATOES IN CURRY SAUCE

Mix

1½ lbs hamburger	2 tbsp chopped parsley
½ cup minced onion	1½ tsp salt
1 cup bread crumbs in ⅓ cup sour cream	¼ tsp pepper

Form into balls 1 inch in diameter. Brown on all sides in skillet with 3 tbsp cooking fat, then remove to a casserole. Brown 20 small potatoes in the same skillet and place them over the meat balls.

Sauce:

1 can condensed cream of celery soup	1 cup sour cream
	½ tsp curry powder

Mix thoroughly and pour over potatoes and meat balls. Cover and bake at 350° for 25 minutes. Uncover and bake 12 minutes longer. Serves 6.

MEAT BALLS IN PUNGENT SAUCE

Mix

1 lb hamburger	1 tbsp Worcestershire sauce
1 lb ground lean pork	2 tbsp prepared mustard
½ cup bread crumbs in ½ cup milk	2 tbsp soy sauce
¼ cup applesauce	1½ tsp salt
2 eggs, slightly beaten	¼ tsp pepper

Form into balls 1 inch in diameter and roll in flour. Brown on all sides in skillet with ¼ cup cooking fat, and remove to a casserole. Mix in a saucepan

1 cup water	½ cup brown sugar
⅔ cup dry white wine	12 cloves
¼ cup wine vinegar	½ tsp ginger
½ cup Karo syrup	

Cover and cook for 6 minutes. Pour over meat balls, cover and bake at 350° for 25 minutes. Mix 1 tbsp cornstarch in 2 tbsp water, stir into sauce, and bake 15 minutes more. Serves 8.

MEAT BALLS WITH RED CABBAGE

Mix

2 lbs hamburger	3 tsp salt
2 eggs, slightly beaten	¼ tsp pepper
1 cup bread crumbs in 1½	¼ tsp nutmeg
cups milk	1 tsp monosodium
⅓ cup chopped raisins	glutamate

Form into balls 1¼ inches in diameter and set aside. Sauté ½ cup chopped onions with 2 tbsp butter in a large kettle. Stir in 3 tbsp flour. Slowly add ⅓ cup wine vinegar, stirring constantly. Add 2 bay leaves and 5 cloves. Cover and simmer for 10 minutes. Add meat balls and simmer 10 minutes longer.

Mix

6 cups chopped red cabbage	2 tsp salt
1½ cups cubed peeled apple	¼ tsp pepper
2 tbsp brown sugar	

Add mixture to top of meat balls, cover, and simmer for 30 minutes. Serves 6.

MEAT BALLS SAUERBRATEN

Mix

1 lb hamburger	1 tsp salt
1 egg, slightly beaten	¼ tsp pepper
¾ cup chopped onion	⅛ tsp marjoram

Form into balls 1¼ inches in diameter and brown on all sides in 2 tbsp butter.

Add

½ 8-oz can tomato sauce	8 gingersnaps
½ cup Rhine wine	8 peppercorns
½ cup wine vinegar	8 cloves
1½ cups water	2 tbsp brown sugar
⅓ cup seedless raisins	1 bay leaf

Cover and simmer for 30 minutes.

Place meat balls in serving dish, strain sauce, stir in ¾ cup sour cream and pour over meat balls. Serves 4.

MEAT BALLS STROGANOFF

Mix

1 lb hamburger	¼ tsp pepper
½ cup bread crumbs	1 tsp monosodium
½ cup milk	glutamate
1 tsp salt	

Form into balls 1 inch in diameter. Brown all sides in 3 tbsp butter and remove from pan.

Sauté for 10 minutes in same pan

1 tbsp butter	½ cup chopped onion
½ lb sliced mushrooms	

Add 2 tbsp flour. Stir in 1 cup condensed beef bouillon.

Add

Meat balls	¼ tsp salt
1 tsp Worcestershire sauce	¼ tsp pepper

Cover and simmer for 20 minutes. Just before serving, stir in ¼ cup sour cream. Serves 4.

MEAT BALLS IN SPICED SAUCE

Mix

1 lb hamburger	1 tbsp minced parsley
1 egg, slightly beaten	1 tsp Worcestershire sauce
½ cup bread crumbs in ½ cup milk	1 tsp salt
2 tbsp minced onion	1 tsp monosodium glutamate
¼ tsp pepper	

Form into balls 1 inch in diameter and roll in flour. Brown in skillet with 2 tbsp butter. Sauté 1½ cups chopped onion in 2 tbsp butter until soft, then add

½ cup blanched almonds	½ tsp cinnamon
⅓ cup seedless raisins	¼ tsp ginger
½ tsp curry powder	¼ tsp salt
½ tsp mace	¼ tsp pepper

Simmer for 20 minutes, add 1 cup hot water and the meat balls and simmer for 20 minutes more. Serve with saffron rice. Serves 4.

MEAT BALLS IN TOMATO SOUP

Mix

1½ lbs hamburger	1 tsp salt
½ cup uncooked rice	¼ tsp pepper
1 egg, slightly beaten	½ cup bread crumbs

Form into balls 1 inch in diameter and place in pan with 1 can condensed tomato soup, then add

2 tbsp chopped green onion	2 tbsp chopped green pepper
½ soup can of water	

Cook slowly for about 1 hour until both meat balls and rice are tender. Serves 6.

MEAT BALLS AND VEGETABLES IN A KETTLE

Mix

¾ lb hamburger	3 tbsp grated onion
¼ lb ground pork	3 tbsp chopped parsley
1 egg, slightly beaten	1 tsp salt
1 cup milk	¼ tsp pepper
½ cup bread crumbs	

Form into balls, roll in flour, and brown on all sides in 2 tbsp hot fat. Place in kettle. Add 2 cups strained tomatoes and 1 tsp Kitchen Bouquet. Simmer for 10 minutes. Add 1 cup hot water, 10 medium carrots, 10 small whole onions, ½ cup chopped celery. Cover and simmer for 30 minutes. Add 1 cup peas and cook until peas are tender. Serves 4.

MEAT BALLS IN VEGETABLE SOUP

Sauté ⅓ cup chopped onions in skillet with 2 tbsp cooking fat. Mix onions with

½ lb hamburger	½ tsp salt
1 egg, slightly beaten	
½ cup bread crumbs in ¼ cup milk	

Form into 12 balls and cool in refrigerator for 45 minutes. In the meantime, mix

1 cup chopped onion	½ cup chopped celery
1 cup raw cubed potatoes	2½ cups tomatoes
2 cups water	½ cup snipped celery leaves
2 sliced carrots	2 tsp salt

Cook in a covered kettle for 30 minutes, then drop meat balls into boiling soup. Cover and simmer for 12 minutes. Serve soup topped with chopped chives and grated Cheddar cheese. Serves 4.

CASSEROLES

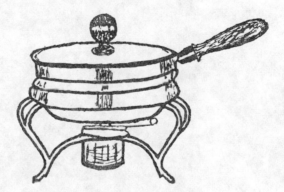

HAMBURGER, BEAN, AND SAUSAGE CASSEROLE

Soak 1 lb dried white marrow beans in water overnight. Drain beans and save the water. Add enough water to make 4 cups. Pour the beans and water into a heavy 4-qt kettle. Add 2 cans condensed beef bouillon. Sauté 2 cups chopped onions in 3 tbsp butter and add to the simmering beans.

Add

2 crushed cloves garlic	1 tbsp salt
½ tsp thyme	½ tsp pepper
½ tsp marjoram	½ tsp oregano

In the same skillet used for onions, sauté ½ lb bulk sausage and ½ lb hamburger. Add meat to the beans and place all in a casserole. Bake at 350° for 1½ hours. Add 2½ cups tomatoes and bake 30 minutes more, or until beans are tender. Stir occasionally. Serves 6.

HAMBURGER CABBAGE CASSEROLE

Place 4 cups of chopped cabbage in the bottom of a greased baking dish. Add ½ tsp salt, ⅛ tsp pepper, ¼ cup water. Cover and place in an oven at 375°. Mix 1 cup bread crumbs, ½ cup milk, ¼ tsp grated lemon rind and beat well with a fork. Mix the crumb mixture with

1 lb hamburger   1 tsp salt
1 cup minced onion   ¼ tsp pepper
1 egg, slightly beaten

Form into a cake the shape of the baking dish and place
on top of the cabbage. Return to the oven uncovered and when the
meat is browned, place slices of American cheese on top and
sprinkle with buttered bread crumbs. Return to oven until cheese
melts. Total baking time, about 30 minutes. Serves 6.

HAMBURGER CHILI CASSEROLE

Form 1½ lbs hamburger into 6 flat patties. On three of them
place chopped canned chili pepper, chopped green onion, chopped
ripe olives, and a slice of American cheese. Cover with the other
3 patties and seal edges. Brown patties in a skillet with garlic
butter, then place in a casserole.

Mix

2 cups mashed canned   1 tsp salt
   tomatoes   ¼ tsp pepper
1 tsp chili powder

Pour over patties and bake at 350° for about 30 minutes.
Garnish with parsley. Serves 3.

HAMBURGER AND CORN CASSEROLE

In 4 tbsp cooking fat, sauté ¾ cup chopped onion and 2
sliced green peppers. Add

1 lb hamburger   ½ tsp pepper
1½ tsp salt

Cook until meat is lightly browned, then remove from fire.
Stir in 2 beaten eggs. Place 1 cup of fresh corn in bottom of
casserole, then half the meat mixture, and top with a layer of
sliced tomatoes. Repeat layers and top with ½ cup of dry bread

crumbs. Dot with butter and bake at 375° for 35 minutes. Serves 6.

HAMBURGER CORN CHIP CASSEROLE

In 2 tbsp cooking fat, brown 1 lb hamburger, ¾ cup chopped onion and ⅓ cup chopped green pepper until meat is crumbly.

Add

⅔ cup chopped cooked ham	½ tsp oregano
1 8-oz can tomato sauce	1 tsp salt
1 tsp sugar	¼ tsp pepper
¼ tsp basil	

Simmer for 15 minutes. Place 1¼ cups corn chips on bottom of casserole, then half the meat mixture, a layer of corn chips, the balance of meat mixture, and top with layer of corn chips. Bake at 350° for 30 minutes. Garnish top with whole corn chips and ripe olives. Serves 6.

HAMBURGER CREOLE CASSEROLE

In 3 tbsp butter, fry 1 lb hamburger, ½ cup minced onions, and ¼ cup chopped green pepper until hamburger is browned, then add

1 cup canned tomatoes and juice	1 tsp salt
½ tsp Worcestershire sauce	¼ tsp pepper

Cover and simmer for about 10 minutes, and then place in a casserole. Spoon small mounds of mashed potatoes on top of meat mixture. Brown under broiler and serve immediately. Serves 4.

HAMBURGER AND EGGPLANT CASSEROLE

In ¼ cup butter or margarine, brown 1 lb hamburger and 2 medium onions, chopped.

Add

1 8-oz can tomato sauce	2 tsp salt
1 cup hot water	¼ tsp pepper
1 tsp sugar	

Peel and slice 1 large eggplant and fry quickly in 4 tbsp salad oil. In a casserole, arrange a layer of eggplant, half the meat mixture, eggplant, and top with the remaining meat mixture. Bake at 325° for 1 hour. Serves 8.

HAMBURGER AND HOMINY CASSEROLE

In 1 tbsp cooking fat, brown 1 lb hamburger, ¾ cup chopped onions, and ½ cup chopped green pepper until meat is crumbly.

Add

1 cup cooked hominy grits	1 8-oz can tomato sauce
⅔ cup condensed beef bouillon	¾ tsp salt
	¾ tsp chili powder

Place in a 2-qt casserole and sprinkle top with ⅔ cup grated Cheddar cheese and ½ cup dry bread crumbs. Bake at 350° for 30 minutes. Serves 6.

HAMBURGER KIDNEY BEAN CASSEROLE

Brown 1 lb hamburger in ¼ cup bacon drippings or cooking fat and add

1½ cup chopped onion	1 tsp chili powder
½ cup chopped green pepper	1 tsp salt
1 minced clove garlic	

Cook for 5 minutes, remove from fire and add 1 No. 303 can tomatoes, 1 No. 303 can kidney beans, and ¾ cup uncooked rice. Mix well and pour into a casserole. Sprinkle with ⅔ cup grated American cheese and ⅓ cup chopped black olives. Bake covered at 350° for 1 hour, or until rice is tender. Serves 8.

HAMBURGER LENTIL CASSEROLE

Soak 4 cups lentils overnight, then boil in salted water for 1½ hours and drain. Fry ½ lb bacon crisp and put aside. Sauté 7 cups chopped onions in the bacon drippings until they are soft and remove. Sauté ½ lb mushrooms in the same drippings until tender and remove. Fry 4 lbs hamburger in same drippings, adding more if necessary. Crumble hamburger as it browns. Mix all ingredients and put in a large casserole. Top with 1 No. 2½ can cooked tomatoes and sprinkle with a generous layer of Parmesan cheese. Dot with butter and bake at 350° for 45 minutes. Serves 10 to 12.

HAMBURGER LIMA BEAN CASSEROLE

Fry 1 lb hamburger with ¼ lb pork sausage until browned. In same fat, sauté ¾ cup chopped onion, ⅓ cup chopped green pepper, and 1 cup mushrooms. Mix all together and add 1 tsp salt. Cook 2 packages frozen baby lima beans and mix with meat mixture. Stir in ½ pint sour cream and place all in a casserole. Spread ½ pint of sour cream over top and sprinkle with 3 tbsp grated Parmesan cheese. Bake at 350° for 25 minutes. Serves 6 to 8.

HAMBURGER, ONION, AND BEAN CASSEROLE

Boil 2 peeled, large onions in salt water for about 30 minutes until tender. Drain, cool, cut in half crosswise and separate the shells. Mix ½ lb hamburger, ½ cup bread crumbs, ¼ cup milk, ¼ tsp sage, ½ tsp salt, and ⅛ tsp pepper. Place this mixture in the large outside onion shells. Chop up the small inside shells and mix with 4½ cups canned baked beans. Place beans in a casserole and push stuffed onions down into the beans. Top each stuffed onion with ½ slice of bacon and bake at 325° for 1 hour. Serves 4.

HAMBURGER AND RICE BALL CASSEROLE

Mix

½ lb hamburger	¼ cup evaporated milk
¼ lb ground fresh pork	½ cup chopped onion
1 egg, slightly beaten	1½ tsp salt
½ cup cold mashed potatoes	¼ tsp pepper
½ cup uncooked rice	¼ tsp poultry seasoning

Form into 8 equal patties and place in large covered baking dish. Mix 2½ cups tomatoes with ¾ cup water and pour over patties. Cover and bake at 350° for 1 hour. Remove cover and bake 30 minutes longer, basting with sauce occasionally. Serves 4.

HAMBURGER SPINACH CASSEROLE

Brown 1 lb hamburger in 2 tbsp cooking fat, add 1 package frozen spinach, cover, and cook until spinach thaws. Stir in 1 can condensed cream of mushroom soup, 2 tbsp soy sauce, ¼ tsp pepper, and ⅓ cup grated Cheddar cheese. Cook until cheese melts, then place in a greased 2 qt casserole. Sprinkle with ¼ cup grated Cheddar cheese and 3 tbsp buttered dry bread crumbs. Bake at 400° for about 10 minutes, or until cheese melts. Serves 4 to 6.

HAMBURGER POTATO STEW

Slice 6 large potatoes in a large baking dish. Cover with 1 lb hamburger, 6 sliced small onions, 4 cups canned tomatoes, 1 tsp sugar, 1 tsp salt, ¼ tsp pepper, and 1½ cups sour cream. Cover and bake at 325° for 1 hour, or until potatoes are cooked through. Serves 6.

HAMBURGER NOODLE CASSEROLE

In 2 tbsp olive oil, brown 1 lb hamburger until crumbly.

Add

1½ cups sliced onions	½ tsp paprika
1 crushed clove garlic	1 tbsp salt
1 No. 2½ can tomatoes	2 bay leaves
1 6-oz can tomato paste	½ tsp Tabasco
1 6-oz can water	⅛ tsp thyme
1 tsp Worcestershire sauce	⅛ tsp marjoram

Bring to a boil and remove from heat. Place half the mixture in a 2½ qt casserole. Add 8 oz uncooked noodles and top with remaining meat mixture. Bake at 375° for 45 minutes. Sprinkle with Parmesan cheese. Serves 6.

HAMBURGER SAUSAGE CASSEROLE

Mix

1½ lbs hamburger	1 tsp salt
¼ lb pork sausage	¼ tsp pepper
¼ tsp poultry seasoning	

Place half of this mixture in the bottom of a casserole, next add 6 small cooked onions and 6 small cooked potatoes. Top with remaining meat mixture. Sprinkle with ½ cup buttered bread crumbs and ¼ cup grated American cheese. Bake at 325° for 1 hour, or until mixture is cooked and top is brown. Serves 6.

BAKED TAGLIARINI

In 2 tbsp olive oil, sauté 1 cup chopped onion, 1 chopped green pepper, 1 minced clove garlic, until tender. Add 1 No. 2½ can tomatoes and cook for 10 minutes. Cook 1 8-oz package noodles according to directions on package. Sauté 1 lb hamburger until crumbly. Combine mixtures and season with 2 tbsp chili powder, 1 tsp salt, and ¼ tsp pepper. Add 1 No. 303 can whole-kernel corn, 1 No. 303 can ripe pitted olives, and 7 oz grated Tillamook cheese. Place in a casserole and sprinkle with 1 oz Tillamook cheese. Bake at 350° for 1 hour. Serves 6.

CHILI PIE CASSEROLE

Put ¾ cup water and 2 tbsp butter in a pan and bring to a boil. Add 1 cup flour and stir vigorously with a fork until a ball of dough is formed. With a fork, knead in ½ cup sharp grated cheese, 1 tsp salt, ¼ tsp paprika and 2 eggs. Refrigerate for one hour. On floured wax paper, form into 12 thin pancakes with floured fingers to prevent sticking. Cool. Brown in a skillet with 3 tbsp cooking oil and drain on paper towels. To make filling, sauté in 2 tbsp cooking oil

1 cup chopped onion	1 minced clove garlic
1 cup chopped green pepper	¾ lb hamburger

Stir in 3 tbsp flour and then add

3 8-oz cans tomato sauce	½ cup chopped ripe olives
1 2-oz can sliced mushrooms	1 tbsp chili powder
1 No. 303 can whole-kernel corn and juice	¾ tsp salt

Bring mixture to a boil, then place in layers in a large casserole, alternating with layers of the pancakes. Top with ½ cup sharp grated cheese and bake at 350° for 30 minutes. Serves 6.

BURGER BALLS AND GREEN NOODLE DINNER

Mix

1 lb hamburger	½ cup tomato sauce
1½ cups soft bread crumbs	1 tsp salt
½ cup chopped onion	¼ tsp black pepper

Form into 24 small balls and brown in a skillet on all sides. Remove from skillet and add to skillet enough butter to make ¼ cup cooking fat. Add ¼ cup flour and blend. Stir in 2 cans condensed beef bouillon and 1 cup of milk. Cook until thick, then add ⅓ cup grated Parmesan cheese, 1 tbsp tomato paste, 1 crushed clove garlic, and ¼ tsp salt. In the meantime, cook 6 oz green noodles according to directions on package. In a casserole, place layers of noodles, meat balls, noodles, meat balls, and top with noodles. Pour sauce over all and bake at 350° for about 20 minutes. Serves 6.

CHINESE HAMBURGER CASSEROLE

Brown 1 lb hamburger without salt and place in the bottom of a casserole. Put a layer of 2 cups diagonally sliced celery on top of the hamburger, then a layer of 1 package of thawed frozen peas. Make a sauce by mixing

¾ cup chopped onion	2 tbsp milk
1 can condensed cream of mushroom soup	2 tbsp soy sauce
	½ tsp pepper

Pour sauce over the peas and top with 1 cup crushed potato chips. Sprinkle paprika on top and bake at 375° for 30 minutes. Serves 6.

EASY HAMBURGER CASSEROLE

In 1 tbsp cooking fat, brown 1 lb hamburger, ¾ cup chopped onion and 2 cloves of finely chopped garlic.

Add

1 No. 2½ (26-oz) can tomatoes	1 lb cooked sea-shell macaroni
2 8-oz can tomato sauce	1½ tsp salt
1 8-oz can water	
1 No. 303 can whole-kernel corn	

Put all in a casserole and bake at 350° for 20 minutes. Stir in 1 cup diced celery and bake 10 minutes more. Serves 6.

VARIATIONS: Add 1 can condensed vegetable soup. Serves 6 to 8.

Substitute 1 lb cooked spaghetti for the macaroni.

MEAT BALL AND NOODLE CASSEROLE FOR FIFTY

Mix

7 lbs hamburger	2 tbsp salt
8 eggs, slightly beaten	2 tsp pepper
2 cups bread crumbs	

Form into balls 1 inch in diameter. Brown all sides in 1 cup cooking fat.

Add

3 cups chopped onion	1 tsp pepper
3 cups chopped celery	2 tsp monosodium
6 No. 303 cans tomatoes	glutamate
2 tbsp Worcestershire sauce	¾ cup sugar
2 tbsp salt	

Cover and simmer for 30 minutes. While meat balls are simmering, cook 4 lbs noodles in salted water for about 7 minutes. Drain and rinse.

Mix 1 cup melted butter and 2 cups flour. Add meat ball mixture, stirring until thick. Serve meat balls over noodles. Serves 50.

QUICK HAMBURGER CASSEROLE

Brown ¾ lb hamburger in 2 tbsp cooking oil. Slice 3 medium potatoes in bottom of greased casserole. Season with salt and pepper. Slice 3 medium carrots on top of potatoes. Season with salt and pepper. Sprinkle ½ cup uncooked rice over carrots. Spread hamburger over the rice. Slice 1 onion over the meat. Pour 2 cups tomatoes over all and top with buttered bread crumbs. Bake at 350° uncovered for 1 hour. Serves 6.

TAMALE CASSEROLE WITH CORN CHIPS

In 2 tbsp olive oil, brown 1 lb hamburger, 1 cup chopped onion, and 1 clove minced garlic. Add

2 8-oz cans tomato sauce	½ cup chopped parsley
1 can condensed beef bouil-	2 tbsp chili powder
lon	1 tsp salt
1 pkg frozen whole-kernel	½ tsp monosodium
corn	glutamate
1 tall can pitted ripe olives	

Heat to boiling point. Stir in 2 3½-oz packages corn chips, remove from heat and cool. Place in a casserole, sprinkle with 1½ cups grated American cheese, and bake at 350° for 1 hour. Serves 8.

VARIATION: Add ½ lb Italian sausage which has been sliced and fried.

ENGLISH HAMBURGER CASSEROLE

In a large size casserole the following ingredients are placed in layers, each layer being seasoned slightly with salt, basil, and thyme. First, a layer of 5 cups cubed raw potatoes, topped with a layer of thinly sliced onions. Brown 3 lbs hamburger in drippings and break into small pieces for the third layer. Place a layer of thinly sliced green peppers on top of the hamburger and top with 1 cup of uncooked rice. Pour 1 can condensed mock turtle soup over the rice and finish off with 1 No. 303 can cooked tomatoes. Cover and bake at 350° for 2 hours. Serves 12.

SAVORY HAMBURGER CASSEROLE

Cook 8 oz macaroni according to directions on package. Brown ½ cup chopped onion, ½ lb sliced mushrooms, and ½ lb hamburger in 3 tbsp cooking fat. Add 1 tsp salt, 1½ tsp paprika, 2 tbsp flour, and blend. Gradually add 1½ cups milk, stirring constantly until thick. Stir in 1 cup sour cream and 3 tbsp minced parsley. Add the drained macaroni. Place all in a casserole and top with ½ cup buttered cracker crumbs. Bake at 375° for 30 minutes. Serves 4 to 6.

TAMALE PIE

In a large skillet with 4 tbsp cooking fat, sauté 2 cups chopped onion, 1 minced clove garlic, and 2 lbs hamburger until meat is browned. Add 1½ tsp salt and ½ tsp pepper. In a large kettle mix 1½ cups yellow corn meal, 1½ cups milk, a No. 2½ can tomatoes, and 1½ tsp salt. Cook slowly for about 30 minutes, stirring often. Add 1 No. 303 can yellow cream-style corn, 1 cup sliced ripe olives, and 2 tbsp chili powder. Mix well, combine the two mixtures, and transfer to a casserole. Bake at 300° for 1½ hours. Serves 12.

MILD TAMALE PIE

Sauté ¾ cup chopped onions in 2 tbsp olive oil. Add 2 lbs hamburger and cook until meat is browned. Add 2 8-oz cans tomato sauce, 1 No. 303 can yellow cream-style corn, 4 tsp chili powder and ½ tsp salt. Cook for 15 minutes. In the meantime, mix 3 well-beaten eggs, ½ cup milk, and 1 cup yellow corn meal. Cook for 5 minutes over a slow fire. Add 1 cup sliced black olives to first mixture and place in a casserole. Top with corn meal mixture and bake at 350° for 35 minutes. Serves 8.

> VARIATION: In place of the corn meal, use 1 package of corn-muffin mix cooked according to directions on package.

RICE TAMALE PIE

Brown 1 lb hamburger in a skillet and drain off fat. Add 4 cups cooked rice, 1 8-oz can tomato sauce, 2 cups condensed beef bouillon, 1 tbsp chili powder, 1 tsp salt, and ½ tsp pepper. Place in a greased 3-qt casserole and sprinkle with 1 cup grated American cheese.

Combine

1 egg	½ cup sifted yellow corn
½ cup milk	meal
2 tbsp vegetable oil	2 tsp baking powder
½ cup sifted flour	2 tbsp sugar
	¼ tsp salt

Mix until smooth and spread over tamale mix. Bake at 425° for 25 minutes. Serves 8.

ITALIAN SPECIALTIES

SPAGHETTI MEAT SAUCE

In 2 tbsp cooking oil, brown ¾ lb hamburger, 1 cup chopped onion, 2 minced cloves garlic, and add

3½ cups sieved canned to-matoes	1 tsp fennel seed
	½ tsp oregano
2 6-oz cans tomato paste	1 tsp salt
2 6-oz cans water	1 tsp pepper
¼ cup minced parsley	

Simmer covered for 3 hours and serve over cooked spaghetti. Serves 6. (Makes 6 to 7 cups.)

RIGATONI

Cook 1 10-oz package of rigatoni according to directions on package. In 2 tbsp cooking oil, brown 1 lb hamburger, ½ cup chopped onion, and 1 minced clove garlic. Add

1 egg, slightly beaten	2 tbsp spaghetti meat sauce
2 tbsp grated Parmesan cheese	(see recipe)
	1 tsp salt
	¼ tsp pepper

Stuff rigatoni with the above mixture and place in a baking dish. Cover with 2 cups spaghetti meat sauce (see recipe) and 2 tbsp grated Parmesan cheese. Cover tightly with aluminum foil. Bake at 350° for 40 minutes. Serves 6.

LASAGNE

Cook 1 lb lasagne noodles according to directions on package, adding ¼ cup cooking oil to the water.

Mix

2 lbs ricotta cheese	⅓ cup chopped parsley
2 eggs, lightly beaten	1½ tsp salt
⅓ cup grated Parmesan cheese	¼ tsp pepper

Drain lasagne noodles and place a layer of noodles in bottom of baking dish. Follow with a layer of ricotta cheese mixture. Sprinkle with a light layer of spaghetti meat sauce (preceding recipe), a layer of thinly sliced mozzarella cheese, and sprinkle lightly with grated Parmesan cheese. Repeat for 5 or 6 layers, and top with lasagne noodles, spaghetti meat sauce, and grated Parmesan cheese. Decorate top with thinly sliced pepperoni. Bake at 350° for 15 minutes. Turn off oven and leave for 5 minutes. Take out of oven and let stand for 15 minutes before serving. Serves 12.

MANICOTTI

Make a pancake batter of

½ cup sifted flour	1 tbsp melted butter
⅔ cup milk	½ tsp salt
2 eggs, well beaten	

Using a small gravy ladle, spoon ladleful of batter into a small hot greased skillet. Tilt skillet around to make pancake as thin as possible. Bake until done on one side only. Slide onto waxed paper and proceed with the next one. Makes about 12 pancakes. To make filling, mix

½ lb ricotta cheese   ¼ cup chopped parsley
1 beaten egg   ½ tsp salt
¼ cup grated Parmesan
  cheese

Spread a spoonful of mixture on each pancake, roll up and arrange in a baking dish. Pour 1½ cups spaghetti meat sauce (see recipe) over top. Bake at 375° for 20 minutes. Serve with additional sauce. Serves 4.

ITALIAN STUFFED EGGPLANT

Sauté ½ cup onions in ¼ cup olive oil. Add

2 8-oz cans tomato sauce   ¼ tsp basil
1 minced clove garlic   ¼ tsp salt
1 bay leaf   ⅛ tsp black pepper
1 tsp sugar

Bring to a boil and simmer for 20 minutes. In the meantime cut a large eggplant in half and cook in salted water until just tender. Drain and scoop out pulp, leaving a shell about ¾ inch thick.

Stuffing:

1 lb hamburger   1 minced clove garlic
Eggplant pulp, chopped   ¼ cup chopped parsley
  fine   2 tsp salt
1 slice bread soaked in milk   ¼ tsp black pepper
1 egg, slightly beaten
3 tsp Parmesan
  cheese

Fill shells with stuffing and place in a large kettle. Surround with peeled potatoes and pour the sauce over all. Cover and cook over a slow fire for about 30 minutes, or until potatoes are done. Serves 4.

ITALIAN HAMBURGER PATTIES

Mix

1 lb hamburger	1 cup finely chopped parsley
¼ cup grated Parmesan	1 tsp salt
cheese	¼ tsp pepper
1 egg, slightly beaten	½ tsp monosodium
1 cup finely chopped onion	glutamate

Form into 16 patties and coat them generously with fine dry bread crumbs. Chill for 1 hour, then fry in cooking oil until done. Serve topped with tomato sauce seasoned with salt, pepper, and oregano. Serves 8.

ITALIAN TINY MEAT BALL SOUP

Mix in a soup kettle

3 cups condensed beef	1 cup chopped celery with
bouillon	tops
2 cups cubed raw potato	¼ tsp oregano
1 carrot, chopped fine	¼ tsp salt
¼ cup canned tomatoes	¼ tsp pepper

Simmer for 30 minutes. In the meantime, soak 2 slices bread in water and squeeze out. Mix with

1 lb hamburger	1 tsp salt
1 egg, slightly beaten	¼ tsp pepper
1 crushed clove garlic	

Form into tiny tiny balls and sauté in 2 tbsp butter. Drop the meat balls and ½ cup fine soup pasta into the soup and cook about 3 more minutes. Serve in bowls and sprinkle with Parmesan cheese. Serves 4.

SPAGHETTI AND MEAT BALLS 1

Mix

1½ lbs hamburger	2 tbsp grated Parmesan
1 egg, slightly beaten	cheese
½ cup bread crumbs	1 tsp salt
¼ cup chopped parsley	¼ tsp pepper
1 minced clove garlic	

Form into balls and brown on all sides in 2 tbsp cooking oil. Make spaghetti meat sauce (see recipe). During the last half hour of cooking, add the meat balls to the sauce. Serve over cooked spaghetti. Serves 6.

SPAGHETTI AND MEAT BALLS 2

Sauté 1 cup chopped onions in 2 tbsp fat until soft. Add 1 lb hamburger and cook until meat loses red color, stirring often.

Add

2 crushed cloves garlic	2 bay leaves
2½ cups tomatoes	1 tsp dried sage
1 chopped green pepper	¼ tsp thyme
2 tbsp chopped parsley	1 tbsp salt
2 6-oz cans tomato paste	¼ tsp pepper
1½ cups water	

Simmer uncovered for 2 hours. In the meantime, mix

¾ lb hamburger	½ cup bread crumbs
1 egg, slightly beaten	¾ tsp cornstarch
½ cup light cream	1 tsp salt

Form into small balls and brown in 2 tbsp cooking oil in skillet. Add meat balls to sauce last 30 minutes. Cook 1 lb spaghetti according to directions on package. Serve sauce over hot spaghetti. Serves 6.

PAESANO SPAGHETTI AND MEAT BALLS

Meat Balls:

1 lb hamburger	½ cup condensed beef
½ lb ground lean pork	bouillon
2 eggs, slightly beaten	½ cup chopped parsley
3 slices whole wheat bread	Grated rind of ½ lemon
soaked in ½ cup milk	⅛ tsp nutmeg
¾ cup chopped onion	⅛ tsp cloves
1 large minced clove garlic	1 tsp salt
⅓ cup chopped green pepper	1 tsp black pepper

Mix well, cover, and chill for 1 hour. Form into balls 2 inches in diameter. Place in a roasting pan with 2 tbsp olive oil and 3 bay leaves. Bake at 450° for 15 minutes, brush with olive oil and bake 15 minutes more.

Sauce:

Fry ¼ lb finely chopped salt pork and 1 minced clove garlic until brown. Add ½ lb round steak cut in small pieces and brown. Add ¼ cup Rhine wine and cook slowly for 15 minutes. Add ⅓ cup chopped parsley, ½ tsp salt, ½ tsp pepper, and ¼ tsp basil. Add 3½ cups canned tomatoes, 1 6-oz can tomato paste, and ½ cup water. Cook for 30 minutes. Add baked meat balls and cook for 1 hour more. Stir occasionally. Pour sauce over cooked spaghetti. Serves 6.

SPAGHETTI WITH MEAT SAUCE

Mix

¼ lb hamburger	½ cup chopped onion
¼ lb minced ham	¼ tsp salt

Fry in a skillet until brown. Add 1½ cups tomato sauce, ¼ tsp salt, ⅛ tsp cayenne and simmer until meat is cooked. Serve over cooked spaghetti. Serves 4.

SPAGHETTI WITH MEAT SAUCE FOR FIFTY

Brown 9 lbs of hamburger and add the following:

1½ lbs chopped onions	⅓ cup Worcestershire sauce
6 qts tomatoes	1 crushed clove garlic
8 cups catsup	1 oz salt
3 bay leaves	1 tsp pepper
2½ qts water	2 tsp cayenne pepper
2 cups chopped green pepper	1 tsp thyme

Stir and simmer until thickened, about 2 hours. Serve with 8 lbs spaghetti cooked according to directions on package. Serves 50.

SPAGHETTI WITH MUSHROOM SAUCE

Put 2 tbsp olive oil in a Dutch oven and sauté the following:

1 cup chopped onion	1 small chopped carrot
½ cup minced parsley	1 whole clove garlic

When onion is soft, remove garlic clove, add 1½ lbs hamburger, cook and stir till hamburger loses color. Add 2 8-oz cans tomato sauce and 1 can hot water. Cook and stir for 5 minutes. Add ½ tsp oregano, 1 tsp salt and ¼ tsp pepper. Simmer, stirring frequently, for 1 hour. Add ½ lb sliced mushrooms sautéed in butter for 10 minutes. Simmer for 1 more hour. Add grated rind of ½ lemon. Serve with 2 lbs spaghetti, cooked according to directions on package. Serves 8.

EASY SPAGHETTI AND MEAT SAUCE

Sauté ⅓ cup minced onion in 1 tbsp cooking fat. Add ¾ lb hamburger and cook until meat loses red color. Add ½ tsp salt, ½ tsp garlic salt, ⅛ tsp pepper, and 1 can spaghetti in tomato sauce. Heat and top with Parmesan cheese. Serves 4.

> VARIATION: Heat 2 cans spaghetti sauce with meat. Combine with 8 oz thin spaghetti, cooked according to directions on package. Add ½ cup sautéed mushrooms and top with Parmesan cheese.

ITALIAN MEAT LOAF

Soak 2 slices white bread and 2 slices rye bread in one cup of milk, mashed with fork. Mix with

1 lb hamburger	3 tbsp grated Parmesan
¾ cup chopped onion	cheese
1 egg, slightly beaten	2 tbsp butter
2 tbsp chopped parsley	1 tsp salt
	¼ tsp pepper

Shape into loaf and bake at 375° for 30 minutes. Top with 1 8-oz can tomato sauce and sprinkle with ¼ tsp oregano. Bake 20 minutes more. Serves 6.

ITALIAN HAMBURGER MINESTRONE SOUP

In 2 tbsp cooking fat, in a large kettle, sauté 1 cup chopped onions and 1 lb hamburger until meat is brown.

Add

1 No. 303 can tomatoes	1 cup sliced raw carrots
1 cup chopped cabbage	¾ cup sliced celery
1 cup raw potatoes, cubed	¼ cup chopped green pepper

Bring to a boil and add

1½ qts water	¼ tsp oregano
¼ cup uncooked rice	¼ tsp basil
2 bay leaves	4 tsp salt
½ tsp thyme	¼ tsp pepper

Cover and simmer for 1 hour. Serve sprinkled with grated Parmesan cheese. Serves 6.

MEXICAN SPECIALTIES

ALBONDIGAS SOUP

Sauté 1 cup chopped onion in ¼ cup vegetable oil for 5 minutes. Add ½ cup tomato sauce and 3 qts chicken stock. When boiling, add 1 cup sliced carrots, 1 lb fresh peas, and ½ lb string beans, cut and sliced. To make the meat balls, mix

½ lb hamburger	¼ cup chopped parsley
½ lb ground lean pork	8 mint leaves
3 tbsp uncooked rice	1 tsp salt
1 egg, slightly beaten	½ tsp pepper

Form into very small balls and drop into boiling soup. Cover and let simmer for 30 minutes. Serve with buttered tortillas. Serves 6 to 8.

MY FAVORITE MEXICAN CHILI

Brown 3 lbs hamburger and 1 cup chopped onions in 3 tbsp cooking fat.

Add

2 6-oz cans tomato paste	1 tsp cuminseed
4 6-oz cans water	1 tsp ground cuminseed
2 mashed cloves garlic	½ oz unsweetened cooking
8 crushed dried red peppers	chocolate
1 tbsp chili powder	

Simmer for 3 hours. Add more water if necessary. Skim oil from top before serving. Serve over cooked spaghetti. Serves 8.

MEXICAN CHILI FOR FIFTY

Mix

13 lbs hamburger (browned)	3 oz salt
2 qts tomato purée	3 oz chili powder
1 lb chopped onions	4 oz ground cuminseed
½ lb suet	Water to make 12½ qts
2 oz unsweetened cooking	volume
chocolate	

Simmer for 3 hours. Add 6 oz flour made into a paste and continue cooking until flour is done. Serves 50.

CHILI CON CARNE FOR FIFTY

Sauté 7 lbs hamburger, 4 cups chopped onion, and 15 mashed cloves garlic in 1 cup cooking fat until lightly browned.

Add

5 qts condensed tomato soup	1 tbsp salt
6 qts red kidney beans	1 tbsp black pepper
6 tbsp chili powder	1 tsp red pepper
2 tbsp cuminseed	

Cook slowly for about 45 minutes. Serves 50.

MEXICAN GOULASH FOR FIFTY

Mix

3 lbs hamburger	6 cups chopped onion
3 lbs pork sausage	2 cups chopped green pepper

Brown in a large heavy skillet and set aside.

To make white sauce, mix

1½ cups of the meat drippings	1 tbsp salt
3 cups flour	1 tsp pepper

Cook over slow heat until mixture bubbles. Stir in 2 qts milk and continue stirring until mixture begins to boil.

Combine

Meat mixture	1½ lbs uncooked macaroni
3 qts white sauce	¼ cup chili powder
3 qts cooked tomatoes	1½ tbsp salt

Cover and simmer for 30 minutes, stirring often. Serves 50.

VARIATION: Place mixture in 4 baking pans and bake at 400° for 50 minutes.

HAMBURGER ENCHILADAS

In 2 tbsp cooking oil, brown 1¼ lbs hamburger and ½ cup chopped onion.

Add

2 6-oz cans tomato paste	1 tsp red pepper
1 12-oz can mixed vegetable juice	1 tsp garlic salt
1 cup water	1 tsp salt
2 tsp chili powder	¼ tsp black pepper

Simmer for 45 minutes. In the meantime prepare ½ lb grated Cheddar cheese and ½ cup chopped onions. Starting with 24 corn tortillas, dip each one in hot fat just long enough to soften it. Drain on a paper towel and spread 2 tbsp meat sauce on each tortilla. Sprinkle with grated Cheddar and chopped onion. Roll up and place in shallow baking dish. Sprinkle tops with remaining cheese and onions and pour 1 cup meat sauce over all. Bake at 350° for 15 minutes. Serve with additional sauce. Serves 8.

MEXICAN STUFFED GREEN PEPPERS

Mix

1 cup hamburger	1 egg, slightly beaten
2 cups cooked rice	1 tbsp Mexene
½ cup chopped onion	⅛ tsp black pepper

Fill 6 cleaned whole peppers and bake at 350° until done, about 40 minutes. Serves 6.

TORTILLA RELLENO

In 2 tbsp cooking oil, lightly brown 1 lb hamburger, ½ cup chopped onion, and 1 minced clove garlic.

Add

1 cup chopped ripe olives	½ tsp chili powder
1 cup drained canned toma-toes	1 tsp ground cinnamon
	⅛ tsp ground cloves
½ cup chopped raisins	1 tsp sugar
2 tbsp vinegar	1 tsp salt

Simmer for 20 minutes, then spread mixture on 12 hot tortillas. Roll up and place in a greased shallow baking dish.

To make sauce, sauté ¼ cup chopped onion and 1 minced clove garlic, in 1 tbsp cooking oil until transparent.

Add

2 8-oz cans tomato sauce	1 tsp chili powder
¼ cup chopped green pepper	¼ tsp oregano
¼ cup chopped celery	⅛ tsp thyme
¾ cup condensed beef bouillon	

Simmer for 20 minutes. Pour half of sauce over tortillas, sprinkle with grated Cheddar cheese, and bake at 350° for 20 minutes. Serve with remaining sauce. Serves 4.

TACOS

Sauté 1 lb hamburger and 1 cup chopped onion seasoned with 1 tsp salt and ¼ tsp pepper. Place liberal portion of meat mixture in center of a folded tortilla and fasten with toothpick. Fry on both sides until crisp, then remove toothpick. Serve with side dishes of shredded lettuce, grated Cheddar cheese, chopped green onion, diced tomatoes, and Louisiana hot sauce. Serves 8.

SOUPS

CHILI CON CARNE AUTHENTIQUE

Sauté 2 cups chopped onions in 4 tbsp beef fat. Add ½ lb finely chopped beef kidney fat and cook slowly until the fat is all rendered. Add 3 lbs hamburger, 2 minced cloves garlic, 1 tbsp salt. Cook and stir until meat is well browned.

Add

2 cans condensed beef bouillon	½ tsp Tabasco
3 tbsp chili powder	½ tsp black pepper
1 tbsp cuminseed	½ oz baking chocolate

Cover and simmer for 2½ hours, stirring frequently. Serves 6.

HAMBURGER LIMA CHOWDER

In a Dutch oven, brown 1 lb hamburger in 2 tbsp cooking fat.

Add

2½ cups canned tomatoes	2 cups diced celery
1 No. 303 can cooked lima beans	1 bay leaf
4 cups hot water	½ tsp garlic salt
1 cup sliced carrots	2 tsp salt
	½ tsp pepper

Cover and simmer for 30 minutes. Remove cover and cook for 15 minutes more. Serve with ¼ cup finely chopped parsley as a garnish. Serves 6 to 8.

HEFTY HAMBURGER SOUP

Sauté 1 cup chopped onion in ¼ cup butter until soft. Add 1½ lbs hamburger and stir until red color disappears.

Add

1 No. 303 can cooked tomatoes	Chopped tops of 4 celery stalks
3 cans condensed beef bouillon	6 sprigs parsley
2 No. 303 cans water	12 peppercorns
1 cup sliced carrots	1 tbsp salt
2 bay leaves	½ tsp thyme

Cover and simmer for 1 hour. Serves 6 to 8.

HAMBURGER SOUP FOR FIFTY

To 3 gallons of meat stock, add

4 lbs hamburger, well browned	8 oz sliced celery
8 oz uncooked rice	8 oz sliced carrots
8 oz chopped onions	12 oz peas

Simmer for about an hour, or until rice is done. Serves 50.

HAMBURGER SOUP

Sauté 3 crushed cloves garlic and 2 cups chopped onions in ¼ cup salad oil until onions are soft, not brown. Add 1½ lbs hamburger and cook over a high heat for 5 minutes, stirring constantly. Add 1 No. 303 can tomatoes, chopped, and 3 cups cubed potatoes, and cook and stir for 5 minutes more. Then add

1 cup condensed beef
   bouillon
2 quarts water

1½ tsp salt
½ tsp pepper

Cover and simmer for 30 minutes. Serves 6.

MEAT BALLS IN ONION SOUP

Mix

1 lb hamburger
¼ cup minced onions
1 egg, slightly beaten
¾ cup oatmeal
½ cup milk

1 tsp salt
½ tsp pepper
½ tsp monosodium
   glutamate

Form into very small balls, brown in a kettle with 2 tbsp drippings. When brown, add 2 cans condensed French onion soup and 1 cup water. Simmer until soup thickens slightly and serve in bowls with croutons and Parmesan cheese. Serves 6.

MEAT BALL SOUP

Mix 1 lb hamburger, 1 slightly beaten egg and 1 tsp salt and form into small balls. Place the following ingredients in a large kettle and bring to a boil:

2 cups diced carrots
2 cups diced potatoes
2 cups canned tomatoes
1 cup chopped onion
5 cups water

1 cup chopped lettuce leaves
1 cup chopped green pepper
1 minced clove garlic
1 tsp salt
½ tsp pepper

Simmer for about 20 minutes and drop meat balls into soup. Cover and simmer for 20 minutes more. Top with chopped parsley and serve in bowls. Serves 4.

DIETETIC MEAT BALL SOUP

Mix 1 lb very lean hamburger, ¼ cup skimmed milk, ¼ cup wheat germ, 1 tsp salt, and form into small balls. Place the following ingredients in a large kettle and bring to a boil:

2 cups canned tomatoes	1 cup chopped lettuce leaves
2 cups diced carrots	1 minced, clove garlic
1½ cups chopped green pepper	1 tsp Angostura bitters
	1 beef bouillon cube
1 cup diced celery	1 tsp salt
1 cup chopped onion	½ tsp pepper
5 cups water	

Simmer for 20 minutes. Add meat balls, cover, and simmer for 20 minutes more. Serve garnished with chopped parsley. Serves 4.

TOMATO CABBAGE MEAT BALL SOUP

Mix

1 lb hamburger	½ tsp salt
1½ slices bread, soaked in ½ cup milk and mashed	⅛ tsp crushed chili peppers
	⅛ tsp sage
½ cup minced onion	⅛ tsp thyme
1 egg, slightly beaten	1 crushed garlic clove

Form into 24 meat balls and place in refrigerator. For soup, pour 1½ qts water in a kettle and add

4 vegetable bouillon cubes	1½ tbsp sugar
1 6-oz can tomato paste	1 tsp salt
1 cup chopped onion	¼ tsp pepper
1 tbsp butter	⅛ tsp crushed chili peppers

Bring to a boil, simmer for 15 minutes. Add 4 cups shredded cabbage, simmer for 15 minutes more. While cabbage cooks, fry the meat balls in 2 tbsp cooking fat until brown on all sides. Add meat balls to the soup and cook 10 minutes more. Serves 6.

SPLIT PEA SOUP FOR FIFTY

Soak 4 lbs split peas overnight, drain, and add

7 qts boiling water	6 tbsp salt
1 lb bacon rind or ham bone	1 tsp pepper
1 cup chopped onion	1 tsp liquid smoke

Cover and boil until peas and onions are tender. Put through coarse sieve, then add enough water to make 8 quarts. Brown 2 lbs crumbled hamburger in drippings or cooking fat until done. Add the hamburger, heat, and stir in 13 cups evaporated milk. Serve hot but do not boil. Serves 50.

VIKING MEAT BALL SOUP

Mix

¾ lb hamburger	¼ cup finely chopped onion
¼ lb ground lean pork	¾ tsp salt
1 egg, slightly beaten	¼ tsp pepper
1 cup milk	¼ tsp allspice
1 cup fine dry bread crumbs	

Let stand in refrigerator for 2 hours to blend flavors, then form into balls 1 inch in diameter and drop into 2½ qts of boiling condensed beef bouillon. Cover and simmer for 20 minutes. Serves 8.

RANCH STEW

In 1 tbsp drippings in a heavy kettle, sauté 1 lb hamburger, 1 cup chopped onions, and 1 cup chopped green pepper until hamburger is browned, stirring occasionally. Add the juice from a 1-lb can whole-kernel corn, 1 No. 2 can kidney beans, and 1 No. 2 can tomatoes and cook until liquid is reduced to about one half. Add the tomatoes, beans, and corn and season with 1¼ tsp chili powder and 1 tsp salt. Bring to a boil and serve. Serves 6.

SAUCES

BARBECUE SAUCE

Mix

3 tbsp butter	2 tbsp brown sugar
½ cup minced onion	2 tbsp prepared mustard
¼ cup minced green pepper	1 tbsp Worcestershire sauce
¾ cup catsup	1 tbsp salt

Simmer for 15 minutes. Serve over barbecued meat. Serves 8. (Makes 1 cup.)

SOUTH SEA BARBECUE SAUCE

Combine in a jar, cover, and shake

½ cup soy sauce	¼ cup brown sugar
3 small pieces gingerroot	2 tbsp olive oil
2 crushed, cloves garlic	¼ tsp black pepper

Baste barbecued hamburgers with this one, or use to marinate steak for 1 hour. Serves 4. (Makes 1 cup.)

TEXAS BARBECUE SAUCE

In a saucepan, heat 3 tbsp bacon fat. Add ¼ cup grated onion and 1 minced clove of garlic. Cook over a medium fire for 2 minutes, stirring constantly. Mix in ½ to ¾ lb finely ground hamburger and cook until meat begins to brown. In a bowl, mix 1 cup catsup, 4 tbsp vinegar, ½ tsp salt, 2 tsp paprika, 1 tbsp prepared mustard, ¼ cup Worcestershire sauce, 1 tsp Tabasco, and 1 tsp chili powder. Add this to the above mixture. Stir constantly over a gentle flame until sauce thickens. Simmer for 15 minutes more. Serve over any meat or fowl. Serves 6. (Makes 2 cups.)

BEARNAISE SAUCE

Cook 3 tbsp chopped green onions in ⅓ cup tarragon vinegar until nearly all the vinegar is absorbed. In a blender which has been warmed with hot water, put 3 egg yolks, ½ tsp dry mustard, 2 tbsp hot water, and blend for 2 minutes. Add the onion, vinegar mixture, and blend. Add, very slowly, ¼ lb melted butter. Serve over hot hamburgers. Serves 4. (Makes 1 cup.)

COLD SAUCE FOR HAMBURGERS

Mix

1 No. 303 can cooked tomatoes chopped very, very fine	2 tbsp wine vinegar
	1 tsp oregano
	2 tbsp olive oil
1 mashed clove garlic	½ tsp salt
¾ cup minced onion	¼ tsp pepper
1 4-oz can peeled green chilies, chopped fine	

Stir well and serve cold over hot hamburgers. Serves 8 to 12. (Makes 3½ cups.)

SPECIAL SPAGHETTI SAUCE

Sauté ½ cup chopped onion in ¼ cup olive oil for 5 minutes or until soft. Add 1 lb hamburger and 2 mashed cloves garlic and stir until meat is browned. Then add

1 8-oz can tomato sauce	¼ tsp pepper
2 cups tomato purée	½ tsp sugar
½ cup chopped mushrooms	Dash of rosemary
¼ cup minced parsley	Dash of thyme
2 tsp salt	Dash of basil

Simmer for 1 hour, add 1 cup dry red wine, and simmer for 1 more hour. Serves 6. (Makes 6 cups.)

MEAT BALLS

MEAT LOAVES

MEXICAN SPECIALTIES

SANDWICHES
AND BARBECUES